Joy to the World!

Copyright © 2025 Robert Boak Slocum

All rights reserved. No part of this book may be reproduced, stored in a retrieval system, or transmitted in any form or by any means, electronic or mechanical, including photocopying, recording, or otherwise, without the written permission of the publisher.

Unless otherwise noted, the Scripture quotations are from New Revised Standard Version Bible, copyright © 1989 National Council of the Churches of Christ in the United States of America. Used by permission. All rights reserved worldwide.

Scripture quotations marked KJV are taken from the King James Version, public domain.

"BCP" texts are drawn from the Book of Common Prayer and Administration of the Sacraments and Other Rites and Ceremonies of the Church, Together with The Psalter or Psalms of David, According to the Use of The Episcopal Church (1979). Scripture texts drawn from the BCP are in the public domain.

Hymn texts are drawn from *The Hymnal 1982: According to the Use of the Episcopal Church* (New York: The Church Hymnal Corporation, 1985).

The poems "Draw nearer Lord" and "Lord we love thee" originally appeared in Robert Boak Slocum, *Seeing & Believing* (2013). Used by permission of Wipf and Stock Publishers, www.wipfandstock.com http://www.wipfandstock.com/.

The poem "Magi" originally appeared in the *Anglican Theological Review*. Used with permission of the *ATR*.

Church Publishing
19 East 34th Street New York, NY 10016
www.churchpublishing.org

Cover design by David Baldeosingh Rotstein
Typeset by Andrew Berry

ISBN 978-1-64065-823-3 (paperback)
ISBN 978-1-64065-824-0 (eBook)

Library of Congress Control Number: 2024947707

Joy to the World!

Devotions for Advent, Christmas, and Epiphany

Robert Boak Slocum

Church PUBLISHING

Contents

Advent Season: Prepare the Way!

1.	Keep awake	3
2.	Prepare the way!	6
3.	Be alert!	9
4.	Day is near	12
5.	The divine potter	14
6.	Heaven comes down to earth	17
7.	No obstacle is too big	19
8.	Bear worthy fruits	22
9.	More powerful than I	25
10.	Trust	28
11.	Rejoicing in the Lord	31
12.	A refiner's fire	33
13.	Leaping for joy	36
14.	Mary's yes	38
15.	Bottom rail on top	41
16.	By faith	44
17.	God with us	47
18.	Serve humbly	49
19.	Seeing and believing	52
20.	The greatest gift	55
21.	Joy comes in the morning	58

vi   Contents

22.	A house of prayer	61
23.	The cosmic order	64
24.	A new temple	67
25.	Nothing is impossible with God	71
26.	Climbing the tree	74
27.	Knocking at the door	77

Christmas Season: Born to Us!

1.	Light has shined in darkness	83
2.	The shepherds' witness	86
3.	Born for us	89
4.	News of great joy	91
5.	Among us	94
6.	A Christmas truce	97
7.	Go, tell it on the mountain	100
8.	Christ shakes things up	103
9.	Love one another	106
10.	Glory to God in the highest	109
11.	Peace on earth	111
12.	The power of humility	114
13.	Waters of abundance	117
14.	In the beginning	120
15.	Love first	122
16.	God's comfort	126
17.	Gleanings of the harvest for the poor and the alien	129
18.	Jesus welcomes the children	132
19.	Jesus' disciples do not fast while he is with them	135
20.	A fisher of people	137
21.	The body of Christ	140
22.	Gifts of mercy	143

Contents vii

23.	Never forgotten	146
24.	A new heaven and a new earth	149
25.	The repairer of the breach	152
26.	The peace of the Lord	155
27.	The peaceable kingdom	158

Epiphany Season: Brightest and Best

1.	Epiphanies	163
2.	The star at its rising	166
3.	The glory of the Lord	168
4.	An incredible catch	171
5.	A great light in the darkness	174
6.	The salt of the earth	177
7.	A covenant with God	180
8.	The creation	183
9.	The true focus	186
10.	The Beloved Son	189
11.	Come and see	192
12.	The good wine	195
13.	Follow me	198
14.	A new teaching	201
15.	Be made clean	204
16.	Not condemned	207
17.	New wine	210
18.	God with us through every danger	212
19.	Knowing Christ	215
20.	Good news	218
21.	Let down your nets	221
22.	A variety of gifts	224
23.	Love your enemies	227

24.	The Word of God fulfilled	230
25.	Transfigured	233
26.	*Get up!*	236
27.	Who is my neighbor?	238
	References	243

Thank you, Victoria Slocum, for helping to prepare this book and your loving patience.

Thank you, Roma Maitlall, for your belief in this project and your careful guidance.

Advent Season

Prepare the Way!

Draw nearer Lord

Draw nearer Lord, you bring new courage
Lighten our path in every day;
Through all our doubts and in our worries
Help us to follow on your way.

Touch all our hearts with your devotion
Open our eyes so we may see;
And in our darkness bring salvation
Until our life is one with thee.

From *Seeing & Believing,*
Robert Boak Slocum

One

Keep awake

"But about that day or hour no one knows, neither the angels in heaven, nor the Son, but only the Father. Beware, keep alert; for you do not know when the time will come. It is like a man going on a journey, when he leaves home and puts his slaves in charge, each with his work, and commands the doorkeeper to be on the watch. Therefore, keep awake—for you do not know when the master of the house will come, in the evening, or at midnight, or at cockcrow, or at dawn, or else he may find you asleep when he comes suddenly. And what I say to you I say to all: Keep awake." (Mark 13:32–37)

Christ comes into our world and our lives, sometimes in unexpected ways or times. Opportunities to discern Christ with us and share his love may arise when we least expect it. Jesus' invitation to "keep awake" urges a way of life, not an avoidance of sleep when we need it. "Keep awake" means to have our eyes open, to be ready, fully alive in each instant. As St. Peter says of the divine voice he heard at the Transfiguration proclaiming Jesus his Son, his Beloved: "You will do well to be attentive to this as to a lamp shining in a dark place, until the day dawns and the morning star rises in your hearts" (2 Peter 1:17–19). Indeed, we do well to be attentive as Christ comes into our world!

Once when working in a hospital, my colleagues and I were heading somewhere to complete an important task, oblivious to our surroundings, when we almost walked past a patient who was sitting on the floor in need of help. Thankfully one of us turned around and noticed him. Though we had an existing agenda, this patient's need was much more urgent. And so, we made a temporary detour so we could help him. One of us was *awake* and ready to respond to the need that suddenly appeared before our eyes.

Likewise, God is present to us and we are present for God, especially if we are awake, alert, available. Every moment is precious. We may find amazing possibilities and great needs if we will only pay attention. That mindfulness means taking in our environment and all the textures of life around us. We may feel the solid earth under our feet and the gentle breeze of the Spirit on our face. There is much to see and hear, and it may touch us deeply if we are engaged, focused, attentive, and not distracted.

Advent is a good time to *keep awake!*

Questions to ponder

1. When has life taken you by surprise?
2. Have you discovered God present in unexpected times or ways?
3. Have you overlooked (or almost missed) something that was really important and right before your eyes?
4. What does it mean for you to keep awake?

Pray with me

Come quickly, dear Lord; be with us. Help us to see you active in our world and in our hearts. Find us in every possible way; surprise us. Open the doors for our ministry and witness, guide us to serve others well. Help us to be alert, present in each moment, ready to see you and share your love.

Two

Prepare the way!

A voice cries out: "In the wilderness prepare the way of the Lord, make straight in the desert a highway for our God. Every valley shall be lifted up, and every mountain and hill be made low; the uneven ground shall become level, and the rough places a plain. Then the glory of the Lord shall be revealed, and all people shall see it together, for the mouth of the Lord has spoken." (Isa. 40:3–5)

Advent can be the most countercultural of seasons. So many people go into a buying frenzy for Christmas, or become anxious that the parties and gatherings will all go well. Christmas music plays in stores from sometime after Halloween. And in the midst of it all, the season of Advent reminds us to slow down, listen, wait, prepare, make room for Christ who comes like distant music drawing closer. Advent brings a certain almost painful yearning for what is to be, but is not yet. "Now I know only in part; then I will know fully, even as I have been fully known" (1 Cor. 13:12).

We may find ourselves counting the days of waiting like separated lovers who will soon be reunited. There is eagerness that comes with expectation

Prepare the way!

and longing that our hope will soon appear, like waiting in the dark for the first light of morning. Every change of light, every instant on the way to a bright sunrise is precious but we need to wait and be patient to see the morning glory as the day changes around us. In a similar way, we need to be patient and expectant with the days of Advent as the season moves at its own pace through its changes toward the day of our hope. Every step has its own beauty, but we will miss it if we rush past. We need to wait with the season, and waiting does not come easily to many of us!

The cultural tension around Advent was very clear on the day of our town's Christmas parade at a church where I served. We had a Saturday evening Eucharist, and the time of the parade coincided with our service time. The church was on the main street of the town so the parade was very near! Inside we added silence to our Advent worship with a spirit of peace, listening for the coming of God's presence among us, preparing the way to our hearts in stillness, lighting the Advent candles of the season. Outside the marching band (with my kids Jacob and Rebecca in it!) would be trumpeting the Christmas holiday with floats and marchers on the way. Santa Claus was coming to town! The contrast was glaring.

Despite all this, I smiled and did not scowl when people offered Christmas greetings in the middle of Advent. Around this time I attended the senior warden's Christmas party. I went outside to see a little of the Christmas parade before the Advent service, and I am sure I waved to my kids Jacob and Rebecca when they passed by with the high school marching band. It was fun. But I also did not want to lose the season of our preparation, for it is easy to miss. Back inside the church, the sounds and lights of the Christmas parade were gone in a few minutes and we carried on. Quietly, expectantly, with great anticipation.

Questions to ponder

1. Do you get impatient? Is it difficult for you to wait?
2. When have you needed to wait for good things?
3. How do you anticipate the coming of Christ into your life?
4. How does Advent make a difference for you?
5. Has anything changed for you during this Advent?

Pray with me

Come, Lord Jesus! Awaken our hope and renew our love. Help us prepare for your advent and welcome you. Fill our hearts with expectation and eager anticipation to know and love you better. Let us be still, listen, and let go of distractions. Help us to wait gently and with patience; let us focus on you.

Three

Be alert!

Now concerning the times and the seasons, brothers and sisters, you do not need to have anything written to you. For you yourselves know very well that the day of the Lord will come like a thief in the night. . . . But you, beloved, are not in darkness, for that day to surprise you like a thief; for you are all children of light and children of the day; we are not of the night or of darkness. So then let us not fall asleep as others do, but let us keep awake and be sober. . . . For God has destined us not for wrath but for obtaining salvation through our Lord Jesus Christ, who died for us, so that whether we are awake or asleep we may live with him. (1 Thess. 5:1–2, 4–6, 9–10)

*S*urprise! The word surprise comes from the French word *surpris,* which means "overtaken." In life, we are often overtaken by situations and events we never expected to encounter. Some surprises may be unwelcome or difficult, but others can be truly wonderful.

A friend of mine was heartbroken to lose a job, but she was surprised and delighted when a better position was offered within a few weeks. She was free to begin a new work and a new direction in her life. She could commit herself fully to this new opportunity. As one door was closing, a better one was opening. And she was ready for it. Her hands were not full—she could welcome her surprise and take a new direction in her life.

God shows up for us at times and in ways we never anticipated or imagined. We may find God's presence overtaking us with love, opening doors we never thought possible, providing comfort, and surprising us with help we never asked for. Our Lord knows us better than we know ourselves. He knows our deepest needs.

Many of us would admit that some of the best things in our lives have come as a surprise—beyond our planning or control. Again and again, we have "just happened" to be in the right place at the right time. The door we needed "just happened" to open when another closed. We "just happened" to hear or see exactly what we most needed to know at the perfect moment. The next chapter of our lives was quietly taking shape before we even realized that the current chapter was coming to an end. It was truly a surprise! And when we are overtaken by grace, we are often left amazed as our horizons and possibilities expand beyond what we ever dreamed.

An "advent" refers to something arriving—something coming into being, a new season, or perhaps the dawn of an entirely new era. It can mean the arrival of a loved one or a friend. Above all, it is the arrival of Christ, and his advent is not just something to be remembered once a year. His coming is daily. He shows up for us in unexpected ways, surprising us with love, gifts, and blessings we did not even know to ask for. He was born into our world, and during this season, we celebrate his miraculous birth.

However, during this season, we also anticipate his final advent, when he will return in power and glory to fulfill and complete all things. Advent is a season rich with surprises. Come, Lord Jesus! Come to us this Advent! Surprise us anew with your grace and your presence.

Questions to ponder

1. Has God ever surprised you?
2. Have you been gifted in ways you never asked for or anticipated?
3. Has God answered your prayers in unexpected ways?

Pray with me

Come, Lord Jesus! Come to us this Advent. Surprise us with your love. Draw near in our best and worst times. Open our eyes so we can see you present, Help us to show up for others who need us. Let us share your surprising love.

Four

Day is near

You know what time it is, how it is now the moment for you to wake from sleep. For salvation is nearer to us now than when we became believers; the night is far gone, the day is near. Let us then lay aside the works of darkness and put on the armor of light. (Rom. 13:11–12)

Wake up! Open your eyes to the world unfolding around you. The time is urgent, brimming with need and aching with possibilities. There is great suffering, yes, but there is also profound love—a love that surrounds us, a love that never falters. God's love reaches out to us, draws near to us, and calls us forward. We can find God with us in all kinds of challenging and difficult situations—whether alone at night in the dark, uncertain about a major decision, or stuck driving in bad rush hour traffic. The Lord is for us, not against us. This divine love is stronger than any force that seeks to divide or destroy. The long night is giving way; the light of day is breaking through.

But the coming of this light does not merely happen to us. Christ's advent is an invitation—a call to awaken, to rise, and to participate in the great work of love and redemption. We are not passive recipients; we are active partners in this story. We say "Amen" with our faith, take risks in love, and offer our hands and hearts in service. In doing so, we welcome God's salvation into the world anew.

Christ's coming is the arrival of a love so transformative that it makes us whole and sends us forth with purpose. We are called to be the voices of his comfort, the arms of his embrace, and the guides who lead others toward the light dawning within our hearts. If we have found the living water, we are called to share it with those who thirst. If we have received the gift of God's love, we must reflect it in our care for those in need. This mission demands our full attention. We must be awake, alert, and engaged to embody and share the new life that Christ's advent brings.

Questions to ponder

1. How do you share the Good News of Christ in your life?
2. What gifts have you received and how do you share them?
3. How does God come to you? How do you know God is present?
4. What helps as you seek God?
5. Do you find God present when you help others,
when you share your gifts, when you love?

Pray with me

God of light and life, draw near when we seek you. Strengthen us for service as you come to us. Let the gifts we receive become the gifts we offer. Be light for our darkness, healing for our pain, inspiration for our lives. Come quickly to help us.

Five

The divine potter

The word that came to Jeremiah from the Lord: "Come, go down to the potter's house, and there I will let you hear my words." So I went down to the potter's house and there he was working at his wheel. The vessel he was making of clay was spoiled in the potter's hand, and he reworked it into another vessel, as seemed good to him. Then the word of the Lord came to me: Can I not do with you, O house of Israel, just as this potter has done? says the Lord. (Jeremiah 18:1–5)

Growth and change go hand in hand. Unlike rocks and dry sticks, living creatures keep on moving and changing. We do not want to be frozen, stiff, or stuck. We want to grow, evolve, become the best version of ourselves.

Changes can be for better or worse. We can seek guidance for our changes and choices. If we are traveling, we want to keep our destination in mind. That would help us to choose our direction and take our next steps. Sharing the fullness of life in God, being at one with our Lord, is our true destination, our completion, our end (Greek, *telos*). In this sense, the end is not just a finish or termination but the completion, the true fulfillment of who we are and are to be. That is our destination in God. When it comes

The divine potter

to our ultimate fulfillment, nothing less will do. The fullness of uninterrupted life and love in God is our end, our fulfillment, our true destination.

And that means changes, lots of them, as we go through our lives growing, discerning, seeking to know God better, trying to live into the promises we have made and discovering the next steps ahead. I remember traveling in the Irish countryside and coming to an intersection with individual pointers and distances to travel for what seemed like every possible destination ("fingers" on a "fingerpost"). There are so many choices! As adults, we carry forward our earlier experiences—good ones and bad ones—in terms of who we have become and what we have learned, and this becomes the starting point for our growth and changes. We may want to build on some experiences, and other situations we may want to avoid. From our mistakes we may discover new goals and destinations along with better ways to approach them and new perspectives on what we are doing, always seeking the One who calls us closer and invites new life.

We do not go through changes alone. God works through us and in us. We may find our Lord present and guiding us through others and in community, through challenges and opportunities we face, in every moment—as we allow it, and participate in the work of God's hands in the pliable clay of our lives. God is the potter, we the clay, shaping and reshaping continually for the sake of his love.

Questions to ponder

1. Who has helped you through important times of change?
2. How have you helped others through times of change for them?
3. Have you known God present in a time of change?
4. Have your changes drawn you closer to God?
5. How may life change for you during this Advent? What guidance or sense of direction do you discern for this season of preparation?

Pray with me

Holy One, guide for our life and lover of souls, be present with us through all our changes. Help us to claim and receive your love. Let us discover our own true selves in you. Gently invite and shape us to know and love you better. You are the potter; we are the clay. Help us to live well in you and help others to know you well.

Six

Heaven comes down to earth

In those days John the Baptist appeared in the wilderness of Judea, proclaiming, "Repent, for the kingdom of heaven has come near." This is the one of whom the prophet Isaiah spoke when he said, "The voice of one crying out in the wilderness; Prepare the way of the Lord, make his paths straight." (Matt. 3:1–3)

It is easy to imagine a great gulf between heaven and earth, with heaven "up there" and everyday life "down here." This separation relegates the life of the Spirit to a "safe" remove above us, out of sight, otherworldly, beyond the clouds. That distance can also leave us feeling disconnected from God's love and the reality of faith. From this perspective, it may seem that we do what we do "here," and God does whatever God does "up there," out of sight and beyond our knowing.

But Jesus comes into our world; he lives in our world. The coming of the Messiah was prophesied and expected before Jesus' birth. John the Baptist steps into this prophetic tradition and expectation with prophecies of his own about the One who is to come. John also stands in the River Jordan where many faithful people will receive from him a baptism of repentance—including Jesus himself. John was the prophet who went before the expected One.

John was the voice crying in the wilderness for preparation and repentance. John announced the coming of the One who ties together heaven and earth, infinite and finite. In Jesus, heaven is near at hand, and God lives with us. In Jesus, humanity is ascended to the life of God. John announces the coming of the one who brings together heaven and earth, the one who brings together divine and human, the one who brings hope for all.

Questions to ponder

1. Has God ever seemed remote from you?
2. Have you come to feel God nearer at times?
3. What brings together faith and daily life for you?
4. What brings together apparent opposites or opponents for you?
5. Have you experienced reconciliation of a disagreement or an injured relationship? What helped?

Pray with me

Blessed are you, Lord God, reconciler and source of forgiveness, who draws us together in love. The pieces of our lives find meaning, connection, and wholeness in you. We open wide our arms and hearts for you. Come quickly. Guide our various paths together and always to you.

Seven

No obstacle is too big

Comfort, O comfort my people, says your God. . . . A voice cries out: "In the wilderness prepare the way of the Lord, make straight in the desert a highway for our God. Every valley shall be lifted up, and every mountain and hill be made low; the uneven ground shall become level, and the rough places a plain. Then the glory of the Lord shall be revealed, and all people shall see it together, for the mouth of the Lord has spoken." (Isa. 40:1, 3–5)

Sometimes obstacles come between us and God; sometimes obstacles come between us and the people who are important in our lives. Obstacles arise in many ways. We all have our own "rough places" and "uneven ground." Maybe we demand too much or accept too little. Maybe we judge without understanding or let misunderstandings grow. Sometimes obstacles can seem permanent, unmovable. But they do not have to be. We can begin to remove whatever gets in the way. We can choose not to carry the heavy things that weigh us down. Some family feuds and disagreements have lasted for years, for generations, with one side or group hurting the other, being hurt, hurting the other again, over and over until someone breaks the vicious cycle. We can let go of old quarrels and obstacles, the things that get in the way.

We can know we are loved and forgiven by God who celebrates every new step to remove the barriers and obstacles. We can forgive and be forgiven. We can begin to find common ground with those who have been distanced from us. We can do our best to make level the uneven ground and smooth the rough places in our own lives—after we admit they exist. Sometimes a disagreement between people can be resolved when we both admit our imperfection; we make mistakes, we can get things wrong. We may be surprised to discover how much we have in common with someone who seems different from us because of appearance, style, or background. As we get to know the person we see before us we may find it easier to let go of our preconceived notions and prejudices about them. I was once walking downtown in a city that was new to me when I encountered someone who seemed like a possible threat at first glance—until I noticed he was pushing a baby in a stroller, lovingly showing the city lights to his small child. I think he may have smiled at me. My first impression was so wrong.

In the light of Christ's advent we can see ourselves, our relationships, and our troubles in a new light. We may be amazed to discover our new vision of God as we remove the obstacles that were blocking our view. We can see the glory of the Lord revealed.

Questions to ponder

1. What are your obstacles to loving God and the people in your life?
2. How do these barriers get in your way? What needs to change?
3. What can you do to remove the obstacles? Can you accept help?
4. Have you overcome obstacles in your own life or seen obstacles overcome in the lives of others?

Pray with me

God of forgiveness and reconciliation, prepare our hearts to know you better and to share your love more fully with others. Forgive us and help us to forgive. Help us let go of whatever obstructs the life we need to live. Open our eyes to see your love active in our lives and around us. Be with us today and always.

Eight

Bear worthy fruits

And the crowds asked John, "What then should we do?" In reply he said to them, "Whoever has two coats must share with anyone who has none; and whoever has food must do likewise." Even tax collectors came to be baptized, and they asked him, "Teacher, what should we do?" He said to them, "Collect no more than the amount prescribed for you." Soldiers also asked him, "And we, what should we do?" He said to them, "Do not extort money from anyone by threats or false accusation, and be satisfied with your wages." (Luke 3:10–14)

John the Baptist foretold the coming new age of the Messiah's advent. This was a time of great change. It meant a new relationship between humanity and God. The door of hope, healing, and salvation was coming open. Light was dispelling the darkness; hope was driving out despair. But this great gift also called for response in faith and action. It was a new way of living in the kingdom of God. This invitation, expressed here by John, draws out our best in terms of who we are and the possibilities of our lives. We do not have to become someone else to share in the coming kingdom. We do not need to look with envy toward anyone else whose gifts or opportunities are different. There is no need to wish we could be them. We can know the life and love of God in terms of our own lives, who we are.

John's advice for sharing the kingdom is flexible, tailored to the needs and capacities of each person. *If* someone has more than enough—clothes, food, whatever—they ought to share with those in need. Tax collectors and soldiers are not excluded from God's kingdom by their work, but they should do their jobs well and fairly. Do not abuse your position, John says. Do not overstep your authority, or twist your position for wrongful personal gain. We can apply that advice to ourselves, whatever our work or daily responsibilities. Using our gifts well, sharing our love and service generously, honoring our own boundaries and those of others—all this leads us into the kingdom of God which is open to us now in terms of who we are and what is possible for us. Christian faith is a life we live. The words of faith translate directly into action.

Questions to ponder

1. How does God's love shape the way you participate in daily life with your family, friends, coworkers, the people you encounter in life?
2. Do your daily actions help you to draw closer to God?
3. Does anything get in the way?
4. What needs to change?

Pray with me

Come, Lord Jesus, open the ways for us to share your life and love. Help us to express our faith in action as we offer ourselves daily and share your gifts. Let us serve you through those who need our help, and guide us to see their need. Help us welcome the advent of your kingdom in this world by our choices and actions.

Nine

More powerful than I

As the people were filled with expectation, and all were questioning in their hearts concerning John, whether he might be the Messiah, John answered all of them by saying, "I baptize you with water; but one who is more powerful than I is coming; I am not worthy to untie the thong of his sandals. He will baptize you with the Holy Spirit and fire." (Luke 3:15–16)

People wondered if John the Baptist was the Expected One, but he pointed beyond himself to the coming Messiah. John was the prophet who prepared the way and told who would follow. John is sent before the Christ; he is not the Christ. John understands his mission and role, including its limits. He is the bridegroom's friend who rejoices greatly when he hears the arriving bridegroom's voice as the bridegroom comes to marry the bride (John 3:29). The bridegroom's friend is delighted and not jealous when the bridegroom and bride are united. John's mission is to herald and prepare the Messiah's coming. The time will come when his work is done.

Our own limitations are also important to understand and respect in every situation. The time may not be right for us to act until another has taken a step or made a decision. Participation in a team or community means that many will have a role to play. We need to leave room for the ministries of others and collaboration. Even (especially) in roles of leadership, we can get in the way if we try to do too much. We need to leave room for others and the surprising gifts they bring, as we leave room for the Holy Spirit who also surprises us. Leaders who try to do everything can burn out quickly while other team members feel left out or excluded. We should also remember that good things may not always happen on our timetable. A person we seek to help may act on a suggestion and start immediately, or at an unknown future time, or never. We may not see the outcome or realization of many good things we have set in motion, or possibilities we have raised. Sometimes we need to let go before the situation is resolved or the story is complete.

We learn from John's selflessness and patience. He has an important role in Christ's coming, but it is not about him. He knows where he stands in the situation. He knows when to let go and make room for the Messiah, the Christ who arrives. John rejoices to hear his voice, and witness his advent.

Questions to ponder

1. Have there been situations or responsibilities when you needed to be engaged fully at one point and let go at another time?
2. Was it difficult to let go or make room for someone else?
3. Have you witnessed times when a refusal to let go caused harm?
4. What helps you to discern when to engage and when to disengage?

Pray with me

Holy One, Lord of our hearts, help us to offer ourselves fully in terms of every gift and opportunity we receive. And help us to recognize our limits in each situation we encounter. Guide us to know when to step up and when to let go. May we always be willing to take appropriate responsibility, to share duties and control as needed, and to turn over responsibility to others when the time is right. Help us to point beyond ourselves to you.

Ten

Trust

Many are saying, "Oh, that we might see better times!" Lift up the light of your countenance upon us, O Lord. You have put gladness in my heart, more than when grain and wine and oil increase. I lie down in peace; at once I fall asleep; for only you, Lord, make me dwell in safety. (Psalm 4:6–8 BCP, 588)

Worry does not help. It does not add an hour to life (Luke 12:25) or solve any problems. Worry can borrow trouble that is not ours. Worry can drain the joy from life. Worry can express fear, lack of trust, need for control.

We have every reason to trust and let go of anxious self-concern. We are written on the palms of God's hands, never forgotten (Isa. 49:16). We are known so well by God that even our hairs are numbered (Luke 12:7). God can "accomplish abundantly far more than all we can ask or imagine" by the power at work within us (Eph. 3:20). Instead of railing against our sad circumstances, we can trust, relinquish our control, and be at peace. God, after all, is with us. Life will go on changing around us, and in us, no matter how hard we try to nail it down or make it fit into our expectations.

We may be surprised to see how well we can adapt when we relax and accept the limits of our power and control.

The peace we are promised is certainly no guarantee that we will get everything we want or hope to have. As St. Ignatius of Loyola says, every life has times of consolation and desolation. There are times when God seems near and times when God seems remote; there are times when we turn to God and times when we turn away (Ignatius of Loyola, *The Spiritual Exercises*). We all face good times and bad times, occasions of joy and satisfaction as well as times of grief and frustration. Some situations that seemed to be the worst may actually lead to the best outcomes in our lives as we overcome adversity; and some situations that seemed the best may actually lead to the worst outcomes with unexpected challenges that emerge. The promise is that in Christ we do not face either the good times or the bad times *alone* (even if we may feel alone). We are never abandoned. Christ is with us, in every dark night, even when we "walk through the valley of the shadow of death" (Psalm 23:4, BCP, 613). Our Lord will also be with us to share celebrations in times of joy. Upheld by Christ and by others in God's name, we know the peace of God. We can dwell in safety, and trust. We are in good hands.

Questions to ponder

1. Have you found Christ present in the best and worst of times?
2. Can you recall a time when faith made a difference for you as you faced an important decision or crisis?
3. Has anyone or anything ever drawn you back to faith at a significant moment in your life?

Pray with me

Blessed are you, Lord God, lover of souls and friend of our hearts, as you surround us with your blessings and stand with us in all our times. Remind us that we are never alone because we have you. Help us find you present with us and share your love generously with others. Let us extend your love widely. Guide us to be light in times of darkness, warmth in times of cold, connection in times of loneliness, encouragement in times of despair. Draw us together in your love.

Eleven

Rejoicing in the Lord

Surely, it is God who saves me; I will trust in him and not be afraid. For the Lord is my stronghold and my sure defense, and he will be my Savior. Therefore you shall draw water with rejoicing from the springs of salvation. And on that day you shall say, Give thanks to the Lord and call upon his Name; Make his deeds known among the peoples; see that they remember that his Name is exalted. (Isa. 12:2–4 BCP, Canticle 9, 82)

I was once the celebrant for a weekday service at a small parish where the altar guild put the cruets of wine and water and the container of bread hosts on a silver tray with a script monogram. I am sure the silver tray was a gift to the parish. The script monogram was three letters, probably the initials of the original owner. As I passed by the tray after the elements for the Eucharist were removed, I glanced at it briefly and misread the monogram. It seemed to say *"Rejoice."* After the service I gave the tray a closer look and laughed at my mistake when I saw only ornate initials in a very fancy engraved script.

But then I thought maybe I got it right the first time. *Rejoice!* It was a good reminder. I could live with it. Rejoice every step of the way. Rejoice because our small group of Christians and friends could be together that day and celebrate our risen Lord. Rejoice in the time to pray and enjoy a somewhat gentler schedule than other days. Rejoice in a beautiful morning. Rejoice because of everything making that day possible; I wasn't taking anything for granted. Rejoice even over my mistake that called to mind a sense of God's nearness, maybe a reminder not to take myself too seriously or rush past a moment in time that was filled with meaning and possibility. Rejoice because we could draw water from the springs of salvation, and share it with thanks.

Questions to ponder

1. When and where have you found joy in your life?
2. When have you found joy in our Lord?
3. Has joy opened your heart?
4. Can you share joy with others and help them to rejoice? Where will you start?
5. How can rejoicing make a difference for you?

Pray with me

Lord of hope and life, giver of grace, move our hearts to rejoice in your love. Guide us when we are troubled, strengthen us when we feel challenged, celebrate with us when we are filled with joy. Let us join your dance. Help us to share your love and rejoice with others. Draw us together in your love.

Twelve

A refiner's fire

See, I am sending my messenger to prepare the way before me, and the Lord whom you seek will suddenly come to his temple. The messenger of the covenant in whom you delight—indeed, he is coming, says the Lord of hosts. But who can endure the day of his coming, and who can stand when he appears? For he is like a refiner's fire and like fullers' soap; he will sit as a refiner and purifier of silver, and he will purify the descendants of Levi and refine them like gold and silver, until they present offerings to the Lord in righteousness. (Mal. 3:1–3)

Advent changes us. It is a journey to be lived. We can be like travelers changed by their travels. By the end of their journey they are not the same people who departed on the trip. T. S. Eliot describes this transformation of travelers in his poem "The Dry Salvages" in *Four Quartets*. He urges "Fare forward, travellers! . . . / You are not the same people who left that station / Or who will arrive at any terminus" (Eliot, "The Dry Salvages," in *Four Quartets*).

The travelers may know they are on a journey but not realize what it will mean for them. They cannot recognize how they will be transformed on the way, or their true destination. Sometimes treatment for a serious illness or injury can begin a journey of faith for the patient in which new insights for life are gained and unexpected growth occurs. Karl Menninger urges that patients can become "weller than well" through treatment—not just returned to a previous baseline but advancing in their own quest for meaning (Menninger, *The Vital Balance*). A crisis of health or any life crisis can be the occasion for new approaches to life and new priorities. We can see with new eyes, claiming unexpected vision and purpose as we proceed in new directions. This can be a journey of faith. We do not have to travel alone.

We wait for God's coming and anticipate God's arrival. God comes to us just as we are but does not leave us just as we *were*. Our Lord is a refiner; we may find ourselves changing as we wait and watch in faith. The advent of Christ gives us light for new perspectives on ourselves and who we are becoming. Our lives can be different because of Christ's coming into our world and our hearts, and we can prepare the way for this. We may be surprised to see what happens if we are open to change and willing to move forward. As we invite Christ into our hearts we may discover Christ is already with us and inviting us to an amazing new life, an unexpected adventure of faith—generous, loving, forgiving, reconciling, transforming, refining.

Questions to ponder

1. What is the dross in us that needs to be refined, burned away, so we may grow in love for our Lord and others?
2. How do we need to change to know Christ better and serve others better?
3. How can we change this Advent?

Pray with me

Blessed are you, Lord God, creator of the universe, lover of souls, you come to us with fire and glory, making our hearts burn with love for you. Refine us! Help us to remove everything, every obstacle that comes between us and you. Help us put aside anything that separates us from you or each other, help us to heal every division that blocks our way. Let us make a new start in this season. Help us find peace in you and each other. Refine the gold of our blazing love for you.

Thirteen

Leaping for joy

When Elizabeth heard Mary's greeting, the child leaped in her womb. And Elizabeth was filled with the Holy Spirit and exclaimed with a loud cry, "Blessed are you among women, and blessed is the fruit of your womb. And why has this happened to me, that the mother of my Lord comes to me? For as soon as I heard the sound of your greeting, the child in my womb leaped for joy. And blessed is she who believed that there would be a fulfillment of what was spoken to her by the Lord." (Luke 1:41–45)

New life wakes us up. I was present for the birth of all three of my kids, and wide awake. It is hard to be dozy or distracted when new life is coming into the world. You want to see it, to know it, to hold it close. When my daughter Rebecca was born I cut the umbilical cord and said to her, "I love you, Rebecca, I love you." She could not understand the words, but maybe she felt the meaning.

With new life we may open our hearts for new love beyond ourselves. New life changes everything—priorities, daily schedules, spending, and goals. In the presence of new life we may feel our limitations, recognize our lack of experience and the smallness of our love. New life means we want to rise to the occasion of this gift, to be our own best self, to live our life better than ever before. Our own giftedness, our potential, the life within *us* may stir with new zeal as new life draws near us—as surely as Elizabeth's baby leaped for joy in her womb as Mary pregnant with Jesus drew near.

A friend of mine described things to be "wild as big deer" when they were exuberant or vibrant, boundless and active beyond all expectations. May our hearts be "wild as big deer" in the presence of new life in Christ. May our Lord find us awake and exuberant at his coming. May our hearts leap for joy as our God draws near us.

Questions to ponder

1. *When have you found new life in others and in yourself?*
2. *When have you been surprised by new life?*
3. *How have your discoveries of new life changed you?*
4. *How can you prepare for new life that is drawing nearer to you?*
5. *How can you share new life with others?*

Pray with me

Holy God, come to us soon and share your life with us. Renew our lives in your grace and glory, transform us with your love. Open our eyes to see you active in our world and lives. Open our hearts for love, compassion, and service. Open our hands for generosity and sharing. Open our minds to know and love you better, and to find you present in all kinds of people and situations. Inspire us to receive your gifts, your love, and every possibility you offer. Let us find new life in you.

Fourteen

Mary's yes

Mary said, "My soul proclaims the greatness of the Lord, my spirit rejoices in God my Savior; for he has looked with favor on his lowly servant. From this day all generations will call me blessed: the Almighty has done great things for me, and holy is his Name." (Luke 1:46–49; BCP, Canticle 15, 91–92)

Mary's words in the Magnificat resound with humility and awe. Mary knows she is a "lowly servant," like each of us, which makes the greatness of God's gift to her and us even more amazing. She rejoices because God has favored her with an incredible gift for us all. She knows this gift exceeds anything she has deserved or earned, and precedes anything she has done. In Mary, we see the perfect example of receiving God's gift with gratitude and surrender.

Like Mary, we are recipients of God's grace. From the very beginning, even before our first breath, God is with us. The grace of God comes first, preceding human action (prevenient grace). We receive life, hope, and salvation as our gift. But receiving the gift demands much from us.

I remember a sign in a veterinarian's office: "Free Cats." It was true. Anyone who asked could take home a kitten free of charge. But there is no free cat, as any cat owner will explain. Even before leaving the office, there were vaccinations and checkups to consider. And once home, our cat needed food, care, and attention. New responsibilities come with the gift. None of this is free. Accepting the gift means to make room for the gift in our lives, to give as we have received, and do what is needed to really accept the gift. Otherwise the gift was never really ours.

In the same way, when it comes to Christ, the gift is free but incredibly expensive to accept. It costs everything—our whole self and life. To receive Christ fully is to make space for Him in our lives, to let His presence shape who we are and what we do. Saying yes to Christ often means saying no to other opportunities, comforts, and pursuits. It is so costly. It requires our whole selves—our love, time, and devotion. Just as Mary gave her entire being in response to God's call, we are called to respond with our whole hearts.

Mary's yes was not passive; it was active and sacrificial. She embraced the gift with openness, knowing it would demand much of her. Her life was forever changed, and through her, the world was transformed.

Questions to ponder

1. Have you given up or turned down one possibility for the sake of something more important to you?
2. Have you received gifts or accepted opportunities that required sacrifices?
3. Has accepting faith caused you to make specific changes or sacrifices in your life?
4. How did this change things for you?

Pray with me

God of mercy and love, strengthen us to accept your gifts and the sacrifices we must make to receive them. Help us to embrace the freedom of your love, and to choose well. Let us respond to love with love. Surprise us with new life that changes everything.

Fifteen

Bottom rail on top

[Mary said, the Almighty] has mercy on those who fear him in every generation. He has shown the strength of his arm, he has scattered the proud in their conceit. He has cast down the mighty from their thrones, and has lifted up the lowly. He has filled the hungry with good things, and the rich he has sent away empty. He has come to the help of his servant Israel, for he has remembered his promise of mercy, the promise he made to our fathers, to Abraham and his children for ever. (Luke 1:50–55 BCP, Canticle 15, 92)

Christ's advent shakes everything up. His mother knew what to expect. The lowly are raised up; weak becomes strong; outcast becomes authority. And vice versa. The powerful and haughty of this world do not hold a power that lasts, but in God the poor and needy are blessed. Woe to the strong of this world who exploit the weak (Luke 6:20–25).

Ken Burns' documentary series *The Civil War* recounts a striking moment when a Black Union soldier confronted his former enslaver, now a Confederate prisoner of war. "Hello, massa," he said. "Bottom rail on top this time." The former slave was free, and the former master was a captive.

The former slave was lifted up and fighting to free others; the former slave owner was cast down, himself unfree. The order of things in the world can change before our eyes. And we can make a difference. Martin Luther King Jr. drew on the words of the abolitionist Theodore Parker to urge that "We shall overcome because the arc of a moral universe is long, but it bends towards justice" (King, "Remaining Awake Through a Great Revolution," National Cathedral, Washington, DC, March 31, 1968).

Christ coming into the world changes everything he touches. St. Paul states that "God chose what is weak in the world to shame the strong; God chose what is low and despised in the world, things that are not, to reduce to nothing things that are, so that no one might boast in the presence of God" (1 Cor. 1:27–29). Christ entering our lives also changes everything, creating in us a new heart (Psalm 51:11), making us free. In Christ, we may give ourselves away generously to serve those in need, to reflect God's love in the world, to build the peaceable kingdom in the way of love.

Questions to ponder

1. *Have you seen established social orders or interpersonal patterns transformed by love?*
2. *Have you seen a society or community changed by love?*
3. *Has love ever changed your priorities or direction?*
4. *Have you come to see any person or group of people differently through a perspective of love?*

Pray with me

God of new beginnings in whom nothing is impossible, make all things new in our lives. Revive us and give us strength for advocacy and service. Let us know you better and reflect your love in the world. Help us overcome every prejudice and hate. Let us turn back every evil and darkness that would tear us down or make us less than you call us to be. Raise us up! Help us to stand and move forward in your power. Guide us to welcome your life coming to us and working through us. Help us to build and strengthen the beloved community in this world. Bring the new day; let it shine brightly in our hearts forever.

Sixteen

By faith

Now faith is the assurance of things hoped for, the conviction of things not seen. Indeed, by faith our ancestors received approval. By faith we understand that the worlds were prepared by the word of God, so that what is seen was made from things that are not visible. (Heb. 11:1–3)

We may feel more keenly the "not yet" of Christ's coming than the "already" of his presence with us as we seek to make sense of our lives and everything that is happening around us. We sense there is "more" for us than we have so far received, and we reach out for God. We listen to discern God's presence with us, and we reach out for help beyond ourselves. This yearning, this reaching out for *more* can find particularly good expression in the season of Advent.

With the perspective of Advent we look forward to the coming of Christ with great hope and expectation. At times this may be a yearning for our Lord's coming that is almost painful. *O come!* We have hopeful signs and prophecies of our Lord's coming, and we prepare. Make the way straight; make the rough places smooth! We are faithful and confident that Christ

By faith

does come and will come to us. But especially for now, in this Advent, our faith is "the assurance of things hoped for, the conviction of things not seen." For now we are expectant, waiting for many things as we look forward to the light of Christ coming into our world. We also await our upcoming celebration of Christmas. It is worth the wait.

Do not be tempted to jump ahead over the season we are *in*. There is unique beauty to be found in Advent that we may not encounter elsewhere in the church year or our lives. Expectant tension can build as we draw steadily closer to the day we celebrate Jesus' birth.

Jumping ahead of the season we are in can be a real loss. I remember when my daughter Claire was nearing the celebration of her sixth birthday. She was very excited about the presents she would receive. She wanted to know what they were! Her mom and I went into a room to wrap the presents and closed the door. Claire knew what was going on, and she could not wait. She wanted to see those presents *now!* So she found a keyhole in the door of the room and peeped through it to see all of her gifts before they were wrapped. She was so glad to know everything she was getting for her birthday until she realized what she had done. There would be no birthday surprise for her. There would be nothing to discover when she unwrapped her gifts. In a sense, opening the gifts would be relatively dull, an anticlimax. She was sad. She could not unsee what she had seen or go back to the time of anticipating her birthday surprises. That was over.

Sometimes waiting can be a good thing. We can look forward to what is coming and what it means to us. We can prepare ourselves and be at our best when the time comes. In this season of Advent we can have the assurance of things hoped for and prepare the way.

Questions to ponder

1. How has this Advent season been a time of preparation for you?
2. Can you find time to be quiet and listen?
3. When have you known God present with you?
4. Are you open to finding God present in new ways?
5. Do you sometimes reach out for God?

Pray with me

Come, Lord Jesus, draw nearer as we wait for you. Lighten our darkness. Awaken hope, strengthen our patience. Remind us you are always with us, even when unseen. Help us find you when we reach out to you. Always call us back to you.

Seventeen

God with us

Seek the Lord while he wills to be found; call upon him when he draws near. Let the wicked forsake their ways and the evil ones their thoughts. And let them turn to the Lord, and he will have compassion, and to our God, for he will richly pardon. For my thoughts are not your thoughts, nor your ways my ways, says the Lord. (Isa. 55:6–8, BCP, Canticle 10, 86)

There is a paradox in faith that becomes acute in Advent: God is with us now, closer to us than we are to ourselves; and yet the relationship is not yet complete for us, not yet fulfilled. We yearn for more, feeling both the distance and the closeness.

Advent offers us a way to engage and live into this paradox. "Now we see through a glass, darkly; but then face to face" (1 Cor. 13:12 KJV). As we wait for the coming of Christ this Advent, we seek the Lord. We are in Christ and eagerly waiting for the coming of the Lord, growing in grace, seeking to know God better, removing obstacles that get in the way, hoping to follow more closely and love more fully. Our eagerness and anticipation can grow with each passing day. We experience the darkness of imperfect union and separation in the predawn darkness of Advent as we eagerly look forward to the new day of Christ's coming. We wait for the dawning of Christ in our hearts.

This is not a game. God wants to be found by us; and we may constantly discover that God has found us first. And yet our knowledge of God with us may always deepen. We may see the reality of God's presence with us ever more clearly as we open our hearts and grow in love. Advent brings new light.

Questions to ponder

1. *How do you seek God? When and how has God found you?*
2. *What reminds you of God's presence in your life?*
3. *Are you waiting for God in this Advent?*
4. *What has changed for you during this Advent?*

Pray with me

Draw near us, good Lord, as we seek to know you better. Bring light to scatter our darkness. Bring hope to brighten our despair. Bring love to warm our indifference. Bring strength to help us when we falter. Guide us forward in loving service, and always closer to you.

Eighteen

Serve humbly

Then Jesus said to the crowds and to his disciples, "The scribes and the Pharisees sit on Moses' seat; therefore, do whatever they teach you and follow it; but do not do as they do, for they do not practice what they teach. They tie up heavy burdens, hard to bear, and lay them on the shoulders of others; but they themselves are unwilling to lift a finger to move them. . . . The greatest among you will be your servant. All who exalt themselves will be humbled, and all who humble themselves will be exalted." (Matt. 23:1–4, 11–12)

Jesus warned the crowds and his disciples against the duplicity of the scribes and Pharisees. They were not worthy of trust or authority, despite their important roles in society. Jesus was not fooled by appearances. In another context he urged his disciples to be "wise as serpents and innocent as doves" (Matt. 10:16).

Things are not always what they seem to be. We may need to look more closely to discover the truth in spite of false or misleading appearances. In a conflict the first-presented concern may not be the real issue, and the genuine conflict will continue to present itself in various forms until addressed. As Christians we are called to be ready to believe, even to give the benefit

50 Joy to the World!

of a doubt—but not to be gullible or easily misled. We may need to draw together many sources and even conflicting perspectives to gain a true understanding of a situation. Solomon faced the dilemma of two women who both claimed to be the mother of a baby. He had the wisdom to discern a way forward and separate the truth from false pretenses (1 Kings 3:16–28). He also had the humility and patience to listen until the whole story with its disagreements was presented. And then he responded decisively to uphold the truth. Deceit was unmasked; truth prevailed.

Authenticity is at the heart of living Christianity. We strive to be authentic, to live in truth and seek it everywhere. Sometimes we may find the truth distorted or obscured; we may need to keep looking until the truth is recognizable. It also helps to acknowledge our own limits and fallibility as we continue to seek and discern the truth. Sometimes we may need to wait and delay action until the truth comes clear in a situation. Advent is a season of waiting to know God's truth more clearly.

Facing the truth about ourselves and others, we do not need to exaggerate or distort. We do not need to present ourselves as more than we are, or accept any misunderstanding of us, because we know our own truth. We know the light of Christ that comes to shatter the darkness, and it is enough.

Questions to ponder

1. What reminds you of your truth—who you are and who you are not?
2. What are the gifts you have received from God or other people?
3. How do your gifts remind you of who you are? How do you share your gifts?
4. When has your discernment helped you to recognize the truth? Have you needed to delay action until the truth came clear in a situation?
5. Have you ever been called back to authentic living as a Christian when you stumbled?
6. Have you encouraged others to authentic living in faith?

Pray with me

Holy God, lover of souls, guide us to be who we claim to be in your name. Let us discern the truth clearly and know when to wait. Help us to live the truth authentically in our lives. Let us remove whatever comes between us and your love. Give us hearts to know the truth and voices to uphold it. Let us also know our own truth and honor it. Remind us of your love and mercy that always surrounds us.

Nineteen

Seeing and believing

> *For we did not follow cleverly devised myths when we made known to you the power and coming of our Lord Jesus Christ, but we had been eyewitnesses of his majesty. . . . So we have the prophetic message more fully confirmed. You will do well to be attentive to this as to a lamp shining in a dark place, until the day dawns and the morning star rises in your hearts. (2 Pet. 1:16, 19)*

In the season of Advent we relive the messianic expectation, the hopeful yearning and watching for the coming of the Messiah into the world. We want to see the Lord more clearly and love him more fully. *O come, Emmanuel! Come and be with us!* We also look forward to the future and ultimate coming of Christ in power and glory. This is the ultimate completion and fulfillment of Christ with us; the end (Greek, *telos*) we are made for. Now we live "between the times," between Christ's first coming and final glory, and we have glimpses of the glory to come in Christ. Sometimes the simplest act of love can provide a glimpse and reminder of God's glory that will be known in its fullness.

At the Eucharist we have a "foretaste of the heavenly banquet," an outward and visible sign of the inward and spiritual grace of God with us, a sacrament. In this way we participate in the life of Christ's body—at one with Christ's incarnate life and ministry on earth, at one with the sacramental body of Christ through the Eucharist, and at one with the church, the body of Christ in the world, as we are individually members of the church (1 Cor. 12:12–13, 27).

Peter, James, and John witnessed a foretaste of Christ's ultimate glory at the Transfiguration (Luke 9:28–36). The "power of our Lord Jesus Christ and his coming" was something real and overpowering that Peter experienced for himself. Peter states he and the others witnessed Christ's transfigured majesty on the holy mountain "with our own eyes." He is not speaking in metaphors, hypotheticals, or "cleverly concocted tales." They saw Jesus transfigured before them in glory: "his face shone like the sun, and his clothes became dazzling white" (Matt. 17:2).

There's a saying among trial lawyers that "one good witness is worth a lot of argument." Peter, James, and John are eyewitnesses of God's glory revealed in Jesus at the Transfiguration—a glimpse of Christ's future coming in power and glory, the final advent and fulfillment of our greatest hope and expectation.

Questions to ponder

1. Have you seen amazing things with your own eyes?
2. Have you been changed by things that amazed you?
3. Was it challenging to share the meaning and beauty of your amazing experience with others? Did they understand?

Pray with me

God of grace, Holy One, reveal yourself to us. Help us to know you present with us. Change us by glimpses of your glory. Let our lives be transfigured by your beauty and love. Overcome us with joy. Help us to be witnesses for the life we find in you; let us share every gift. Draw us always closer to you.

Twenty

The greatest gift

[Jesus said,] For God so loved the world that he gave his only Son, so that everyone who believes in him may not perish but may have eternal life. Indeed, God did not send the Son into the world to condemn the world, but in order that the world might be saved through him. (John 3:16–17)

.

Christ comes into our world and our lives to share love, hope, forgiveness, inspiration, and salvation. Christ does not come shaking a finger at us to condemn our failures and shortcomings. God treats us better than we deserve. Christ enters our world to share abundant life and lift us up, not to humiliate or tear us down.

Sin is often its own punishment. A driver who is reckless, a student or worker who neglects their responsibilities, a partygoer who overindulges—all may face consequences in the natural order of events for what they have done or not done. But these consequences flow from their own choices and actions, not the hand of the Almighty adding an extra weight of divine punishment and condemnation to their burden.

Christ brings new possibilities and hope to us with his advent. Our salvation is based on grace we accept by faith—not on a legal system of just fines and punishments. Christ comes to us in love, seeking to share and restore life. Like the father in the parable of the prodigal son, Christ does not have to sort out right and wrong, good and bad, and every sin before welcoming the troubled son or daughter home (Luke 15:11–32).

Love comes first for the father—love that rejoices in his son's return to life and home. Making the punishment fit the crime is not the father's concern; he does not berate or demean his son. The father goes out to meet his returning son and gives him the best robe; they have a big party to celebrate (Luke 15:20–24).

But the older brother feels mistreated by the prodigal son's warm reception. The older brother had worked faithfully at home for many years and he was never given such a celebration. The father assures the older son of his love, and explains they had to celebrate because his younger brother "was dead and has come to life; he was lost and has been found" (Luke 15:32). Celebrating the prodigal son's healing and new life *is* the father's priority; he does not focus on the punishment of his son's guilt.

The father's mercy and welcome for his prodigal son is good news for us. God is not a distant critic, ready to condemn and punish, excluding all but the most perfect from the kingdom of heaven. Our Lord opens the door wide to welcome and forgive all who step through and accept the blessings of his love. Christ invites us to put our lives in order, to come to terms with our mistakes, to forgive others and ourselves, and to accept forgiveness. Christ comes to surround us in love, to share hope and life eternal, to welcome and include us.

Questions to ponder

1. Have you seen times when forgiveness and compassion were a better way to approach a failure than guilt and condemnation?
2. How can we remove obstacles to our own forgiveness and our forgiveness of others?
3. Do you see a connection between your forgiveness of others and the forgiveness you receive from God?
4. Has God's love or the love of another person helped you to make important changes in your life?

Pray with me

God of love and hope, bless us with healing and forgiveness. Inspire us to share the gift of love that we receive abundantly from you. Help us to forgive others and ourselves as we have been forgiven by you. Guide us to see our first priority is always to love. Help us to see others in the light of your love. Guide us to welcome and include those who differ from us instead of condemning them. Let us know your love better as we share your love with others.

Twenty-One

Joy comes in the morning

Weeping may spend the night, but joy comes in the morning. (Psalm 30:6 BCP, *621)*

Waiting is not easy. Waiting with hope is easier because there is something to wait for; but the temporary separation from hope's completion can be painful. When will our hope be realized? When will it come? Sometimes in the middle of darkness we do not know when there will be light. It may be impossible to tell when (or if) an illness will resolve or a crisis will pass. There may be no guarantee of a good outcome, and all assurances may seem hollow.

We may be eager for morning to come, but at least we know what the new day will look like and when to expect it. We just have to wait. The dawn will break; we will see the sun. But in the darkness of pain, loss, confusion, or grief we do not know when the end of that darkness will come or how to recognize it. We may feel depressed—helpless, hopeless,

Joy comes in the morning 59

worthless, sad. "Weeping may spend the night." In the middle of a storm we may lose our sense of direction, feel overwhelmed, see no way out and no way forward. Like Noah and the others on the Ark during the flood, we may feel rudderless, wondering how long the downpour will last and where we are going (Gen. 7).

Christ comes to us, God is with us, when we feel broken. We find peace and wholeness in the love of God that surrounds us—gathering the fragments of our losses and disappointments into a comprehensive bond of love that enfolds and surrounds us. As James DeKoven noted in a sermon, the fragments of our lives are gathered up and made whole in Christ (DeKoven, "Gathering the Fragments"). The answer to our brokenness is Christ, in whom "we live and move and have our being" (Acts 17:28).

Christ comes into our world and lives. He comes in this Advent to share the best and worst of our experience, redeeming it all. He has known it all before. In Christ our suffering ends; our brokenness is made whole. Our meaning and purpose become clear. Our divisions can be set aside; we can forgive and be forgiven. We can let go of the darkness in ourselves and others.

The dawning of a new day can be wonderful to see. The sky brightens, the darkness fades, colors and finer details begin to appear. Our perspective begins to change and the way forward seems clearer. Christ comes into our world and changes everything. In this light we discover new possibilities of hope, forgiveness, inspiration, and mission. Joy comes in the morning.

Questions to ponder

1. Have you felt overwhelmed, lost in darkness?
2. What helped you to move through this time?
3. Where was the light for you? How did you know that light?
4. Have you known the light of Christ in a time of darkness? Does this light bring a new perspective for you?

Pray with me

God of light and life, come quickly to help us. Lighten our minds and hearts. Guide us to discover hope and new possibilities in you. Give us energy to move past doubt and confusion. Help us to stand; walk with us as we move forward. Let us enjoy each new day with you. Brighten our path; share our joy.

Twenty-Two

A house of prayer

Jesus entered the temple and began to drive out those who were selling and those who were buying in the temple, and he overturned the tables of the money changers and the seats of those who sold doves; and he would not allow anyone to carry anything through the temple. He was teaching and saying, "Is it not written, 'My house shall be called a house of prayer for the nations'? But you have made it a den of robbers." (Mark 11:15–17)

If we want to become available for a new way of life, we may need to put new things together, to find new combinations, to begin a new practice, or start a new work. At times we may need to remove something from our lives that is proving to be a hindrance or obstacle to faith as we seek to "make straight in the desert a highway for our God" (Isa. 40:3). We need to remove anything that comes between us and our Lord, anything that obstructs our vision of God with us. We may have to be quite ruthless about this.

Jesus says we need to be "wise as serpents and innocent as doves" (Matt. 10:16). If something threatens to turn us away from faith or blocks our love of God, if there is something between us and our Lord, we must respond

62   Joy to the World!

decisively. We need to put our house in order as we prepare for the coming of our Lord in this Advent.

Jesus was certainly ready to act without hesitation to remove the money changers and dealers and their customers from the temple. They were corrupting it. Jesus' action expressed his love for God, his mission in the world, the temple, and the people who would worship in "a house of prayer for all the nations" (Mark 11:17)—not a house of trade for profit.

Nothing less than God will do for our worship and ultimate devotion. Our hearts are restless until they rest in God, as St. Augustine states in *Confessions*. Sometimes the most dangerous and seductive idols are not presented as objects for worship like the golden calf made by the people of Israel when Moses ascended Mount Sinai (Exod. 32). Sometimes the most dangerous idols are attractive, perhaps good in themselves up to a point, even greatly needed—but they are not God, and not worthy of our worship. The Temple "market" (or the profits to be made there) became a kind of idol in its day, displacing God in the holy Temple.

When Jesus is fasting and tempted by Satan in the wilderness, the tempter urges Jesus to worship the wrong thing by commanding stones to become loaves of bread. Jesus' need for food to satisfy his hunger is natural, a good thing in itself—but not God. Jesus was not having it (Matt. 4:1–4). Jesus does not succumb to the temptation to idolize his need, as noted by James Griffiss ("Meditations on the Idols of our Temptation," in *A Silent Path to God*). We may be tempted to treat our own needs for money, advancement, reputation, comfort, or admiration as idols worthy of our ultimate homage. These needs are not worthy of our worship.

An automaker once proudly (if humorously) advertised "This car will save your soul." It will not. And it was a great car. My family bought a used version of it, and the car handled well. It was fun to drive and had many safety features. But there was no salvation to be had from that vehicle. Sometimes we lose perspective with our values and practices. We may love what should be used, and use the people we should love. We may need to reset our compass to chart new directions as we prepare for the Lord of heaven and earth who comes to us this Advent.

Questions to ponder

1. Do your lived priorities align with your values? What do you value most?
2. Is there anything less than God that you treat like God?
3. Can you identify any idols in your life?
4. Have you made any changes as you prepare for the coming of the Lord this Advent?

Pray with me

Lord God, creator of the worlds, lover of our souls, help us to prepare for your coming in this season of Advent. There is no substitute for your love. Help us to remove anything that obstructs or hinders our love for you. May our lives reflect the love we know in you. Let our every choice and action express our devotion for you. Be with us through every change, walk with us in every step as we find our way more closely to you. Help us to love others with the love you share.

Twenty-Three

The cosmic order

Glorify the Lord, every shower of rain and fall of dew, all winds and fire and heat. Winter and summer, glorify the Lord, praise him and highly exalt him for ever. Glorify the Lord, O chill and cold, drops of dew and flakes of snow. Frost and cold, ice and sleet, glorify the Lord, praise him and highly exalt him for ever. Glorify the Lord, O nights and days, O shining light and enfolding dark. Storm clouds and thunderbolts, glorify the Lord, praise him and highly exalt him for ever. (Song of the Three Young Men, 42–51; BCP, Canticle 12, 88)

The glory of the Lord brings light and life to the world and our hearts. We see God's glory in the majesty and beauty of nature in all its many varieties. Wind, rain, bright sun, cold, hot, dew, and snow—nature points beyond itself to our creator, the origin and source of all life and beauty reflecting at its best the order and purposiveness of God. All creation is a good gift of our loving God, who works in and through the material world for the redemption of all people and all things.

We do not need to escape from creation to find God; we can find God through creation in the world where we live. Nature can reflect the majesty, power, and beauty of God. We pray for the coming of God's kingdom "on

The cosmic order

earth as in heaven" (BCP, 364). Nature reminds us there is much that is above and beyond us, even as we learn more and more about this amazing creation we share. Julian of Norwich urges that "the fullness of joy is to see God in everything; for by the same power, wisdom, and love with which he made all things, our good Lord is continually leading all things to the same end and he himself shall bring this about; and when the time comes we shall see it" (Julian of Norwich, *Revelations of Divine Love*).

Our encounters with nature can humble us, and remind us of our deep connection with all that goes out from God in the creation of all things, and all that returns to God in the redemption of all things (Latin, *exitus et reditus*). William Blake reminds us that "Everything that lives is holy!" and the new Jerusalem will include "even Tree, Metal, Earth & Stone" (Blake, "Visions of the Daughters of Albion" and *Jerusalem*).

Advent is seen in nature as new light comes into our world in each new day. The darkness is scattered as the brightening light appears. We can see more clearly. We can make a new start, a new beginning in life. Today, our present, *this day* is brand new. Christ comes to us constantly to transform the darkness of our confusion and discouragement. New light awakens new hope and a world of possibility.

Questions to ponder

1. When have you marveled at the beauty of nature?
2. Have you been humbled by the expanse of a night sky with stars, a vast ocean, mountain heights, rugged plains, deep canyons, mighty rivers, cascading waterfalls, a brilliant sunrise, or other showings of nature's beauty and glory?
3. Does the beauty of nature remind you of God's presence? How do you feel in the midst of God's creation?

Pray with me

Holy God, maker of spring's new growth and the colors of fall, source of winter's cold and summer's warmth, shower us with your grace, lift our eyes to the stars. Let your clouds thunder and your waves roar, touch us with the gentle breeze of your devotion, comfort us with the light of your love. Paint in the sky the dawning of a new day as we eagerly await your Advent in this season and in our hearts. Help us to be good stewards of your creation and share every gift you provide. May our love be strong as a river, tall as the trees, quick as deer, constant as the earth.

Twenty-Four

A new temple

And all the people responded with a great shout when they praised the Lord, because the foundation of the house of the Lord was laid. But many of the priests and Levites and heads of families, old people who had seen the first house on its foundations, wept with a loud voice when they saw this house, though many shouted aloud for joy, so that the people could not distinguish the sound of the joyful shout from the sound of the people's weeping, for the people shouted so loudly that the sound was heard far away. (Ezra 3:11–13)

The people of Israel celebrated their return from exile, the Babylonian captivity, as expressed in Psalm 126:1–2: "When the Lord restored the fortunes of Zion, then were we like those who dream. Then was our mouth filled with laughter, and our tongue with shouts of joy" (BCP, 782). Ezra describes the celebration when the foundation was laid for the Second Temple in Jerusalem that would take the place of the First Temple that had been destroyed. It was a moment of great joy, but also a moment of grief and sadness for those who remembered the First Temple. Perhaps what they saw was different from what they remembered, less than their

68 Joy to the World!

hopes or expectations. Whatever they may have hoped, it was clear the First Temple was gone forever. Weeping and shouting for joy were heard together in a great sound on that day.

Sometimes holding too tightly to a memory of the past can interfere with our experience of wonder and discovery in the present. Israel came through the time of exile and once more they would celebrate their faith in the Jerusalem Temple. But it would be different. The situation would be different. The people would be different. The building would be different, perhaps significantly different from the memories and hopes of some. Their grief was understandable. But their loud disappointment was also an obstacle to full and joyous participation in a new chapter in the life of their faith community.

It was a time of great joy and relief for many when the conditions of the pandemic improved enough to lift the lockdowns and restrictions on public worship. In my parish we came back together on Easter Sunday 2021, with a beautiful outdoor service for our first Eucharist after the worst of the pandemic. It was like a resurrection from the dead for our hearts, a new birth for those who had not prayed in person with a congregation or shared Communion for some time. And yet, as we moved forward from that day, there were some who could not or would not return. Our numbers in church were down relative to the time before the pandemic, and some fondly mentioned earlier times years ago when the church was full. The church they found on return was not what they remembered.

We continued to find ways to adapt as the situation changed. None of this was expected or planned for in advance and much of it was certainly different from anything we had seen before—online services, masks, social distancing, limits at times on particular activities (*e.g.,* shared meals, shaking hands at the Peace) that seemed risky. But for the most part, in spite of some differences along the way, we carried on. A dedicated core of parishioners kept things going. We found new ways to do very old things, the practices of our worship and faith. We found ways to "sing to the Lord a new song" (Psalm 98:1 BCP, 727).

Advent is the season for us to be watchful and waiting for God to do a new thing. Jesus' coming into the world was certainly a new thing; and his coming to us is always new and renewing, alive and life-giving, never stale. To celebrate the beauty of our Lord entering the world and our lives, to live into renewal in Christ every day, we can release (or at least carry lightly) our expectations for exactly how this will happen—how we will find and know our Lord present in every day. Christ's advent and renewal may come to us in unexpected ways, blessing us, healing us, and also surprising us.

Questions to ponder

1. Have you grieved the loss of a familiar and important place or situation in your life?
2. In time were you open to new places or situations and able see their importance for you?
3. Have you found or been found by God in unexpected ways?
4. Has your life taken unexpected turns that you came to appreciate more fully in time?

Pray with me

Blessed are you, Lord God, always active in our world and our hearts. You encounter us and stir us up in unexpected ways. Let us see your power and playfulness, and know your love that comes to us in so many ways. Guide us to let go of anything that blocks our vision of you. Renew us; make us new in your love. Let us share an adventure of faith with you for life. Give us strength for the journey and hope. Be with us through every change.

Twenty-Five

Nothing is impossible with God

The angel said to [Mary], "The Holy Spirit will come upon you, and the power of the Most High will overshadow you; therefore the child to be born will be holy; he will be called Son of God. And now, your relative Elizabeth in her old age has also conceived a son; and this is the sixth month for her who was said to be barren. For nothing will be impossible with God." Then Mary said, "Here am I, the servant of the Lord; let it be with me according to your word." (Luke 1:35–38)

Expect the unexpected with God. Our Lord will surprise us with opportunities, new directions, and possibilities we might never have imagined. Mary was certainly not expecting the angel to appear that day with God's invitation for her to carry and give birth to the Son of God. It is likely she could foresee the many obstacles she and her son would face—suspicions, misunderstandings, sneers, resentment. Accepting the invitation would mean a totally changed life for her, a new direction she did not ask for or seek. But she said the yes of faith—she was willing and eager to step into an unknown future that no one had faced before. Although Mary was the favored one, she stepped forward humbly, as a servant, in faith. It must have seemed so impossible, startling, and unexpected—but nothing is impossible with God. She was present and accepting for all God's promises: "Here am I."

Grace surprises us. Sometimes our most significant opportunities will be the most unexpected. We may encounter surprising invitations to begin a new life, stepping into a new role or place or situation. We can listen with our hearts for guidance beyond ourselves to discern whether any unexpected offer or new possibility is a good step for us. Advent is a good time for new beginnings. If we find the calling true and the surprising next step to be good but difficult, we can remember that all things are possible with God.

Questions to ponder

1. How did you discern whether a new possibility was a good step to take?
2. Did you hesitate to take an important but very different or unexpected step because of the challenges you would face?
3. What helped you to adjust to a very new situation? What did you discover?

Pray with me

O Lord, Holy God, our times are in your hands. Guide us to know you better and discover our best paths to you. Help us to use our gifts; let us find new ways to praise you and serve others. Always draw us nearer to you. Give us strength and courage to take every step that leads to you. Share the adventure of new life with us. Be with us through every change, every discovery, every new day in the dawning light of your love.

Twenty-Six

Climbing the tree

[Jesus] entered Jericho and was passing through it. A man was there named Zacchaeus; he was a chief tax collector and was rich. He was trying to see who Jesus was, but on account of the crowd he could not, because he was short in stature. So he ran ahead and climbed a sycamore tree to see him, because he was going to pass that way. When Jesus came to the place, he looked up and said to him, "Zacchaeus, hurry and come down; for I must stay at your house today." . . . Zacchaeus stood there and said to [Jesus], "Look, half of my possessions, Lord, I will give to the poor; and if I have defrauded anyone of anything, I will pay back four times as much." Then Jesus said to him, "Today salvation has come to this house. . . ." (Luke 19:1–3, 8–9)

Zacchaeus' life changed when Jesus came to Jericho. Before Jesus came, Zacchaeus seems to have been a crooked tax collector who abused his power to defraud others and enrich himself. People knew he was a sinner. Zacchaeus does not seem to have been loved or respected by the people who knew him.

After Jesus came, Zacchaeus had new life. He promised to give half his possessions to the poor and pay back fourfold anyone he defrauded.

Climbing the tree 75

People grumbled when Jesus visited him; but on that day salvation came to Zacchaeus' house. Jesus "came to seek out and to save the lost."

Zacchaeus' conversion to a new life began before his solemn promises to give to the poor and repay fourfold the people he cheated. It was before he welcomed Jesus to his house, before Jesus recognized him in the tree and invited him to come down to visit. It was before Jesus even spoke to him, before Zacchaeus perched in a sycamore tree to watch and wait for Jesus. Something was moving in Zacchaeus' spirit at least by the time he ran ahead of the crowd gathered to see Jesus. Zacchaeus' heart was already opening by the time he reached for the first branches to climb into the sycamore tree to see Jesus as he passed that way. Zacchaeus, a chief tax collector in the city of Jericho, probably spent very little time climbing trees on most days. This may have been Zacchaeus' first time to climb a tree and stay there since he was a child. Something was moving him.

Zacchaeus knew Jesus was coming to the place where he lived. Zacchaeus likely could not anticipate everything that would change for him because of Jesus' visit, but he was hopeful. He waited to see Jesus and watched for him eagerly. Zacchaeus was glad to see Jesus approach, to accept his invitation, to welcome him in. The advent of Jesus to Jericho changed everything for Zacchaeus. Salvation came to his house; generosity came to his life.

We can share Zacchaeus' experience during this Advent season. We can rejoice to see our Lord drawing near and approaching us. We can wait patiently and watch eagerly for the coming of Christ. We can open our hearts.

Questions to ponder

1. How does Jesus come into your life?
2. How does the presence of Christ make a difference for you?
3. Do you watch for Jesus' approach during this Advent season?
4. Does Jesus' advent change how you relate to others?

Pray with me

Blessed are you, Lord Christ, Holy God, you bring light for our darkness, comfort for our pain, guidance and direction when we are lost, hope for our despair. We eagerly wait and watch for you during this Advent. We welcome you to our homes and lives. Give us new hearts; transform us with your love. Walk with us as we make a new beginning. Let us share your love in the world.

Twenty-Seven

Knocking at the door

Listen! I am standing at the door, knocking; if you hear my voice and open the door, I will come in to you and eat with you, and you with me. (Rev. 3:20)

When I was a very young child someone gave me the children's book *If Jesus Came to My House* by Joan C. Thomas. I think I may have tried to imagine the moment, the situation presented by the author in the title. The premise of the book raises a very important question for daughters and sons of Jesus of all ages—how do we respond when Jesus shows up knocking at our door? What comes next, how do we express ourselves, what changes for us because he came knocking?

Advent is a time for waiting and watching, but it is also a time for action. Jesus comes to our world and to us, bringing new light and hope. But we must respond. Our Lord comes to us and knocks on our door. He comes in love as our savior, our closest family member, our best friend, our beloved visitor. He knocks and patiently waits for our response. He says, "Behold, I stand at the door, and knock" (Rev. 3:20 KJV). But the door must be opened from the inside. Jesus will not force open the door of our hearts. He will be there if we accept him. And he will continue to knock, persistently inviting us to share his life.

We tend to think of Advent as a season when *we* wait on the coming of the Lord, as we do. But Advent is also a season when Jesus waits on us. He will wait as long as it takes. He claims us as friends and does not treat us as slaves or servants (John 15:15). We are his family, his blood relatives. He will not try to frighten, manipulate, or guilt us into a positive response to his invitation of love. Some who claim to represent our Lord may have tried those tactics, but they are ineffective.

Our response of love must be freely given to be real—and it is only real love that Jesus seeks from us. A criminal with a weapon can force my obedience: "Give me your money or else!" But a criminal with a weapon cannot force my love: "Love me or else!" It does not work that way. Real love is a gift, never coerced or forced.

Jesus offers us his life, the amazing life of love shared by the Son in union with the Father (John 17:20–21). We share that love through him. Being at one with our Lord, we share his union with the Father and the Holy Spirit in the dynamic life of the Trinity. As St. Athanasius states, God became human in Jesus so we can share the divine life (Athanasius, *On the Incarnation*). Jesus presents a staggering offer to us when knocking at our door. But we must accept it, receive it. We must open the door for our Lord who knocks this Advent, and always.

Questions to ponder

1. Does Jesus knock on your door?
2. What does it mean for you to open the door? How do you respond?
3. What changes for you when Jesus comes to your house?
4. Have you waited for the coming of Christ during this Advent? Has our Lord waited for you during this Advent?

Pray with me

Come, Lord Jesus, lover of souls, author of our salvation. Draw us near. Come quickly! We wait for you with hope and expectation, and gladly open the door of our hearts for you. Share your life with us and we will dwell with you. Bring light to our darkness. Surround us with your love and we will share it generously in your world. Draw us together so we may all be one with you and each other.

Christmas Season

Born to Us!

Lord, we love thee

Lord, we love thee, always be
In our hearts and minds to see
All our gifts have come from thee.
Lord, we love thee, help us see.

Lord, we love thee, nearer be
Never let us fail to see
Every day we walk with thee.
Lord, we love thee, help us see.

Lord, we love thee, constantly,
Filling all our hearts to see
Life and hope will come from thee.
Lord, we love thee, help us see.

—From *Seeing & Believing*,
Robert Boak Slocum

One

Light has shined in darkness

The people who walked in darkness have seen a great light; those who lived in a land of deep darkness—on them light has shined. (Isa. 9:2)

Today is the day. The promise is true. We see it with our own eyes when we share the love around us. There is new life in humble places—in a stable of animals, in a manger full of hay! There is new life in us. God comes to be with us. God is closer to us than we are to ourselves. God's Son, fully divine and fully human, shares our humanity. Jesus embraces all our vulnerability, birth and death, in an imperfect world where things are out of control and go wrong. And in this imperfect world things can also go right.

If we open our eyes we may be surprised to see amazing new life that transforms us. We can see a great light in a land of deep darkness. Our Lord shows up in our world and *lives*. God is *for us* in the everyday moments of our lives—in good times and bad times, whether we hurt or need or rejoice. God is with us, bringing new life to us, in all our humble places. And the

84 Joy to the World!

gifts we receive can become the gifts we offer. The overflowing generosity of God in this moment can be reflected in our generosity for others; the abundant love of God in this moment can be seen in the love we share.

Christmas will surprise us. I can remember my own excitement as a child when the time for Christmas would come nearer and nearer until Christmas Eve and then the day! There was a parishioner at a church where I served who decorated her Christmas tree for the day and went to bed. The next morning she was very surprised to discover the tree was still decorated, but all the ornaments had moved! During the night her young son removed the ornaments and played with them in his room while everyone else slept. He played with each of the ornaments like a sacred treasure, and eventually put everything back on the tree—but not exactly where he found them!

And yet somehow he got it right. He knew something important was happening. It was worth staying up for, worth getting up for in the middle of the night. It was something he wanted to see for himself, something to touch and hold with his own hands. And even if his arrangement of things was a bit off, he honored the tree, he honored the day, and he honored our Lord with each ornament.

Questions to ponder

1. How is Christmas different from other days of the year for you?
2. How does Christmas move you?
3. Does anything change for you at Christmas?
4. Can you continue these changes through the year?
5. When have you shown up in love for someone else? When has another shown up in love for you? What gifts can you share?

Pray with me

Dear Lord, let your love be born in us today. Make our hearts your home. See how we welcome you! See how we need you! See how we are lost and cold without you! Bring your abundant life into our hearts today. Let today be the new birth of your love in us! Help us to share your love generously.

Two

The shepherds' witness

When the angels had left them and gone into heaven, the shepherds said to one another, "Let us go now to Bethlehem and see this thing that has taken place, which the Lord has made known to us." So they went with haste and found Mary and Joseph and the child lying in the manger. When they saw this, they made known what had been told them about this child; and all who heard it were amazed at what the shepherds told them. But Mary treasured all these words and pondered them in her heart. The shepherds returned, glorifying and praising God for all they had heard and seen, as it had been told them. (Luke 2:15–20)

The angel told the shepherds "good news of great joy" about the new birth of the Messiah in Bethlehem (Luke 2:10–11). And then the shepherds witnessed a multitude of angels praising and offering glory to God. The shepherds hurried to see for themselves the newborn child who was the Expected One. When they saw Jesus and Mary and Joseph, they gave witness to what the angel told them about the child. Mary treasured the shepherds' words and "pondered them in her heart," perhaps helping her realize the enormous gift she received and what just happened.

After witnessing with their eyes and ears the angel's announcement of great joy and the multitude of angels praising God, the shepherds became witnesses for all present at the nativity manger concerning "what had been told them about this child." They amazed everyone who heard them with their witness. The shepherds themselves seem to have been transformed by what they witnessed, "all they had heard and seen," and praised God as they returned to their work.

Witnesses—those who see and hear what happened—can *give witness,* and *become witnesses* who tell the story of what they saw and heard. A witness in a trial gives testimony under oath in open court to put into evidence what they know to be true. In the context of faith, we can witness God active in our world and lives. We may see how our lives have been changed by Christ's activity and presence with us. We may see how we have been forgiven, healed, nurtured, encouraged, inspired, and sent with mission. Like the shepherds in the Nativity story, we may find ourselves transformed and renewed by everything we have come to know in faith—moving us to glorify and praise God as we tell our story.

Questions to ponder

1. When have you witnessed something important? What did you see?
2. When have you been a witness and told others about something important that you saw or knew?
3. Have you witnessed God active in your world and life?
4. Have you been a witness for your faith? How can you share your experience of faith with others?

Pray with me

Holy Lord, God of grace and glory, open our eyes to see you moving in our world and lives. Show us the wonders of your love and help us to share everything we have come to know in faith. Renew our hearts, transform our lives. Help us to be good witnesses for your grace and sing your praises.

Three

Born for us

For a child has been born for us, a son given to us; authority rests upon his shoulders; and he is named Wonderful Counselor, Mighty God, Everlasting Father, Prince of Peace. (Isa. 9:6)

Our Lord comes to us in the power of life stronger than death, love stronger than hate, hope stronger than despair. God's love does not overpower us. We find the greatest strength in vulnerability, availability, willingness to collaborate and cooperate, openness to change for a better way. We know God's powerful love as we listen and learn, forgive others and ourselves, share what we have received, and grow to receive even more.

Instead of posturing, we can claim our lives in vulnerability and deep need for our Mighty God. As we offer ourselves to God in faith we discover life that is most truly our own.

God is with us to make things right between us and God and between each of us. Christ brings the peace of forgiveness, reconciliation, and healing. God comes with power not to coerce or intimidate but to overcome whatever divides us and open the door for life and love that will never be taken away from us. Christ comes for us and our salvation, for our sake, to share God's life and love together. The birth of this child is new life for us.

Questions to ponder

1. When have you felt powerless?
2. Have you received help when you needed it?
3. When have you offered help for another when they needed it? What difference did it make?

Pray with me

Holy One, eternal Son, you are our Wonderful Counselor, you are the Prince of Peace. Always bring us new life; draw us forward in your love. Be the light that brightens our darkness. Help us share your love in this world.

Four

News of great joy

In that region there were shepherds living in the fields, keeping watch over their flock by night. Then an angel of the Lord stood before them, and the glory of the Lord shone around them, and they were terrified. But the angel said to them, "Do not be afraid; for see—I am bringing you good news of great joy for all the people: to you is born this day in the city of David a Savior, who is the Messiah, the Lord. . . ." (Luke 2:8–11)

The herald angel's first words to the shepherds are assurance: Do not be afraid. It is easy to be fearful in times of uncertainty or confusion. We worry when things seem to be spinning out of our control. Our fears can build on each other and our scared thoughts can race ahead of us. Fear can blind us to the amazing good things that surround us and the love of God reaching out for us.

Fear can be unreasonable. I remember a night when my daughter, Claire, was about five years old. A loud bang from our gas heater startled her awake, feeding into a nightmare about a bad wolf lurking in her room. Her piercing cry was filled with terror. When I got to her, Claire was not going to be reasoned out of her fear. No amount of explanation could convince her that no wolf was hiding under her bed. But it was possible to assure her. Over the next few days, we took our "wolf hunts" in her room, with her small hand gripped tightly in mine. We checked under the bed, in the closet, behind the door. Finally she laughed and the spell of her fear was broken. She could sleep easy again.

God's presence in our lives is like that reassuring hand—stronger than fear. The angels brought assurance for the shepherds who were understandably stunned by their direct encounter with God's words and will as announced by the angels. The shepherds had to let go of many assumptions about how things were and what was possible. It must have been overwhelming. But there was no cause for alarm. The angels did not intend to frighten or intimidate. They brought good news of great joy for all. *Fear not!* The angels brought love and hope to overcome fear; they provided assurance. The shepherds' fear gave way to great joy. They were among the first witnesses of the new life in Christ we now share. Christ with us means do not be afraid.

Questions to ponder

1. Have you discovered Christ present for you when life seemed out of control?
2. Have you found guidance in a moment of confusion or fear?
3. Has faith helped you through a time of unexpected transition or loss?
4. Has love helped to overcome your fear? How?

Pray with me

Holy Lord, may your joy strengthen our hearts in every challenge we face. May your love cast out every fear that threatens us. May your assurance give us peace. Encourage us with your near presence in our lives. Let your beautiful life be born in us. Give us peace.

Five

Among us

And the Word became flesh and lived among us, and we have seen his glory, the glory as of a father's only son, full of grace and truth. (John 1:14)

During Advent many of us sing "O come, O come, Emmanuel" with hope for the coming of Christ. It is one of the most beautiful Advent hymns. It expresses yearning, longing, even a kind of sadness in our current distance from the Expected One, as "captive Israel . . . mourns in lonely exile here until the Son of God appear" (Hymn 56, v. 1). Until the Christ comes to us we all mourn in our own versions of lonely exile. We wander in darkness.

The words of this Advent hymn express our plea for God to be with us and take away the pain of separation. But that changes when Emmanuel comes to us—this Christmas and always. Emmanuel means "God with us" (Hebrew). Jesus is born, the Christ comes into the world, the Lord is with us, the Word was made flesh (John 1:14).

God, the maker of heaven and earth, gives up much (divine self-emptying, *kenosis*) to share our humanity (Phil. 2:6). The divine Son becomes human and shares our life so we can fully share God's life and love. Jesus experiences birth, growth, hunger, pain, love, joy, and death—in human terms. Fully human and fully divine, Jesus was seen and heard, showing us how to live holy lives of grace and challenging us to use our gifts to glorify God and participate in the divine life. Jesus was the "pioneer and perfecter of our faith" (Heb. 12:2), humanly opening a way for us to follow and share salvation. This is good news for us, as we pray in "O come, O come Emmanuel" that Christ, "the key of David," will "come, and open wide our heavenly home, make safe the way that leads on high, and close the path to misery" (Hymn 56, v. 5).

The exuberant joy of Christmas displaces the quiet longing of Advent as a brilliant sunrise dazzles and surpasses the dim first light of morning. Heaven and nature can sing; we can "repeat the sounding joy" to celebrate "the wonders of his love"! "Joy to the world! The Lord is come" (Hymn 100, vv. 1, 2, 4). On this and every Christmas we celebrate God with us, God's glory revealed. Christ comes to us to remove the pain of separation and draw us together in love.

Questions to ponder

1. *Have you felt lost in pain and separation from others?*
2. *Do you miss being with important people in your life at this time?*
3. *What helps you to feel connected with others?*
4. *How have you experienced God with you?*
5. *Have others helped you to know God present? How can you share the brightness, love, and hope of this Christmas with others?*

Pray with me

Blessed are you, Lord Christ, Son of the Father, you bring light to our darkness, hope to our despair, and joy to our hearts. Be with us always. Open our eyes to see you present. Guide us to share your love in our world and help others to know you better. Bind us together. Help us to stand, strengthen us for service, let us always walk in the light of your love.

Six

A Christmas truce

Though I walk through the valley of the shadow of death, I shall fear no evil; for you are with me; your rod and your staff, they comfort me. You spread a table before me in the presence of those who trouble me; you have anointed my head with oil, and my cup is running over. (Psalm 23:4–5 BCP, 613)

The Allied and German soldiers shared an incredible Christmas surprise on the western front of Europe in 1914. Despite expectations and hope that World War I would be over by the first Christmas of the war, the fighting continued. The armies were stuck, stalemated, and the war dragged on. Life was miserable in the trenches of both sides. The enemies were in shouting distance of each other. The lines of battle were separated only by a killing field, a "no man's land."

Everything changed at Christmas when the fighting armies made their own truces all along the western front. It was not the generals or the national leaders who initiated this, but the frontline troops. At one place the Allies saw the German soldiers hold up a Christmas tree. It was not an attack. In another place, the soldiers on both sides sang Christmas carols.

Joy to the World!

Instead of killing each other, soldiers along the lines met in the middle of the killing field to exchange small gifts, play soccer, bury the dead. The allied soldiers found their enemies to be very much like themselves, despite wartime propaganda that described the Germans as barbarians.

In *Silent Night,* Stanley Weintraub records one British soldier's report of a Christmas day meeting of enemies. Private Rupert Frey said of their Bavarian opponents that normally "'we only knew of their presence when they sent us their iron greetings.' Now, 'from all sides,' they gathered 'as if we were friends, as if we were brothers. Well, were we not, after all!'" Weintraub also recalls a poem about the Christmas truce by the Scottish poet Frederick Niven that ended: "God speed the time when every day / Shall be as Christmas Day" (Weintraub, *Silent Night*). Unfortunately the truces ended after Christmas, at somewhat different times, and World War I continued with more years of brutal fighting, suffering, dying. But there was peace in "no man's land" for a brief time at Christmas in 1914.

I once taught about the 1914 Christmas truce in a college theology class at Marquette University. I mentioned that the basis for one of the truces along the front lines was prepared a few days before Christmas when the Germans invited the opposing British to share a ceasefire of one hour in honor of their captain's birthday. Instead of throwing a weapon into the opposing trench, they threw a carefully wrapped chocolate cake! It was a tasty invitation. One of my students chose the Christmas truce for his class presentation, and he brought a chocolate cake to share with everyone. We should all eat that cake (Slocum, "Christmas Trees and Chocolate Cake," in *Seeing and Believing*)!

Questions to ponder

1. This Christmas can we stop hurting each other?
2. Can we let go of the quarrels that separate us? Have you found peace in a situation of conflict?
3. Have you helped to de-escalate a fight or resolve a misunderstanding?
4. Have you found common ground with someone who seemed hostile? When?
5. Can you hear and appreciate the perspective of someone who disagrees with you? Can you reconcile with someone who has been an enemy?

Pray with me

Most loving God, bring peace into our hearts and into our world. Help us to love one another as you love all of us. Help us to appreciate our differences and find common ground. Help us to reconcile. Guide us to find ways to work together. Strengthen us to face our challenges with empathy and concern for each other. Surprise us with your grace and let us find unexpected ways forward. Draw us together in peace.

Seven

Go, tell it on the mountain

The heavens declare the glory of God, and the firmament shows his handiwork. One day tells its tale to another, and one night imparts knowledge to another. Although they have no words or language, and their voices are not heard, their sound has gone out into all lands, and their message to the ends of the world. In the deep has he set a pavilion for the sun; it comes forth like a bridegroom out of his chamber; it rejoices like a champion to run its course. (Psalm 19:1–5 BCP, 606)

There is an African American spiritual that urges us to "Go, tell it on the mountain" (Hymn 99), share the news that Jesus Christ is born. *Tell it!* That is what we do with good news. We can "Lift every voice and sing till earth and heaven ring!" (Hymn 599) There is no need to be shy about the good news of our greatest hope. *Shout it!*

We can dance like David and all the house of Israel "were dancing before the Lord with all their might, with songs and lyres and harps and tambourines and castanets and cymbals" in the presence of the Ark of

God (2 Sam. 6:5). We can sing God's triumph in our lives as Moses and the Israelites sang to the Lord after the Red Sea crossing: "I will sing to the Lord, for he has triumphed gloriously. . . . The Lord is my strength and my might, and he has become my salvation" (Exod. 15:1–2). We can share Miriam's song of triumph with dance and tambourines (Exod. 15:20–21). Like the Hebrews, who celebrated the Red Sea crossing and the deliverance of Israel from bondage in Egypt, we have much to celebrate!

If you saw a great movie, visited a superb restaurant, found a wonderful vacation spot, won an award—you would tell your family, friends, maybe even strangers. Something happens to make a good day, and it is even more fun when you share it. Someone else can hear your good news and perhaps share your happiness. Why hide it or keep it to yourself? This Christmas we have the very best news. There is new life and plenty for all. We can declare the glory of God; we can share a sound that has gone out into all lands, a message to the ends of the world.

Questions to ponder

1. When has someone told you their good news?
2. When have you shared your good news with others?
3. How did you feel when you shared good news?
4. Did it make a difference for someone? Does the Good News of Christ make a difference for you?

Pray with me

Blessed are you, Lord God, the new life and clear light of our world. Make us ready to share your love; surprise us. Open our eyes to see you with us. Open our hearts and minds to know you better. Open our lives to serve others generously. Let us share the good news of our life in you; let it begin with us.

Eight

Christ shakes things up

His mercy is for those who fear him from generation to generation. He has shown strength with his arm; he has scattered the proud in the thoughts of their hearts. He has brought down the powerful from their thrones, and lifted up the lowly; he has filled the hungry with good things, and sent the rich away empty. (Luke 1:50–53)

Our God shakes things up. Instead of overlooking the poor and needy, God raises them up. Instead of deferring to the rich and powerful, God overturns their dominance. Instead of bowing to the established orders of this world, Christ reveals a greater power in the way of love, humble service, generous compassion, and ready forgiveness. This was always a threat to the rulers and moguls who wanted power and control for themselves and were ruthless to keep it. Christ in the world threatens the established order of things and questions our power, priorities, and values.

Even as a very young child, Jesus was a fearful threat to those in power. King Herod "and all Jerusalem with him" were frightened when the wise men came asking for "the child who has been born king of the Jews." Herod slaughtered children who were two years old or under in and around Bethlehem for fear a boy that age would come to threaten his rule (Matt. 2:1–16). But Herod was unable to find and kill Jesus who would live to claim a kingdom that was "not from this world" (John 18:36), a kingdom of love, where we are all his equals, his friends, and members of his body.

We celebrate Christ who comes to us with mercy and compassion, but the fulfillment of God's promises also comes with questions for us. Our Lord challenges our self-centeredness and our grasp of truth. Are we transformed by the many gifts we have received in Christ? Can we look beyond ourselves to the needs of others? Is the love of Christ visible in our generosity for those around us? Is it possible for this Christmas season to change our lives? What will be our best gift this Christmas? God always has more for us to discover and share.

Questions to ponder

1. How do we share the blessings we have received?
2. How do we treat the people who need us?
3. How does the birth of Christ make a difference in your life? Do you discover God with you?
4. Does God's presence challenge your habits, attitudes, or prejudices?
5. What has changed for you because of faith?

Pray with me

Most holy God, draw us near and help us share your love in the world. Help us see you and know ourselves truly in you. Help us change and grow as we hear your call and follow you. Give us courage to make a difference. Let us know your peace.

Nine

Love one another

Let anyone who wishes take the water of life as a gift. (Rev. 22:17)

Christmas is more than a party, a holiday, a shopping spree, a day, or a season. God comes into our world in the flesh and changes everything, opening a path for life that lives, hope that inspires, love that shares, generosity that cares and helps.

The good news of Christmas includes the truth that we can change, although the peace of Christmas may be challenging for us as we live it every day. This Christmas gift is free but not easy or cheap. Accepting the gift means we give everything for it; we discover a new way of living. Charles Dickens describes a beautiful and enthusiastic change of heart at Christmas in his "ghostly" novella *A Christmas Carol*. After the miserly character Scrooge has been visited by the ghosts of Christmas past, present, and yet to come, and after he has recognized the consequences of his coldhearted actions, he comes to see his life in a dramatically new way at Christmas.

Scrooge shows concern for others and he wants to share with them. He wants to be included instead of excluding everyone from his life. He becomes generous. He immediately buys the prize turkey at the nearby poultry shop and sends it to his underpaid and overworked clerk, Bob Cratchit, and his family. Instead of coldly dismissing the celebration of Christmas as "humbug," Scrooge is filled with emotion and shows his feelings. He laughs and cries in the same breath. He is joyful: "I am as light as a feather, I am as happy as an angel, I am as merry as a school boy. I am as giddy as a drunken man. A merry Christmas to everybody!" (Dickens, *A Christmas Carol*)

Dickens' story of Scrooge's change of heart is synonymous with Christmas for many people and it is frequently dramatized at this time of year. Maybe there is a little bit of Scrooge in all of us, and we love to see him come to life. The story does point to a truth: hearts can open and lives can change on the day and in the season of Christmas.

Like Scrooge, *we* may be amazed to find enormous joy and energy as we claim new life. Scrooge is delighted when he realizes it is Christmas morning and he is not dead. It is not too late for him to live, and it is not too late for us! We can celebrate God with us and share love that pours out for others. See how we can love one another as we are loved so well by God. It is water for thirsty souls. It is light in the darkness. It is our Christmas present.

Questions to ponder

1. What is the most important gift you can receive this Christmas?
2. What is the best gift you can give?
3. How is Christ's life born in you?
4. How are you made new in Christ?
5. What is changing for you in this Christmas season?

Pray with me

Come into my heart, Lord Jesus. Come and make me new. Come to heal my wounds. Come and raise me up. Come with hope to strengthen me; come with love to guide me. Draw me forward to serve and share. Come into my heart, Lord Jesus.

Ten

Glory to God in the highest

And suddenly there was with the angel a multitude of the heavenly host, praising God and saying, "Glory to God in the highest heaven, and on earth peace among those whom he favors!" (Luke 2:13–14)

We can see God's glory in our world if we open our eyes. Do you see it? Do you hear it? Christ comes to *us*, entering our world to save us. The Christmas story is not just a sentimental tale or a history lesson. God is with us constantly in the present. In God we can find peace on earth.

The Christmas hymns are fun to sing, but they also remind us that Christmas continues for us beyond the event of Jesus' birth and the annual holiday. We continue to witness and share his glory. In "O Little Town of Bethlehem" (Hymn 78), Philips Brooks prays the Holy Child of Bethlehem will be born in us today, and promises "where meek souls will receive him, still the dear Christ enters in."

In "O Come, All Ye Faithful" (Hymn 83), John Francis Wade invites us to "bend our joyful footsteps," changing direction to join the shepherds adoring the newborn Christ. In "It Came Upon the Midnight Clear" (Hymn 89), Edmund H. Sears urges humanity to "hush the noise and cease your strife" to "hear the angels sing," looking forward to a time of peace when all the world will "give back the song which now the angels sing."

The Christmas story continues in our lives today in what we can see, hear, and do. God's life with us continues, and our celebration continues. We can welcome our Lord's coming, refocus our lives to adore our savior, and give back to share the divine love we receive.

Questions to ponder

1. When have you seen God's loving presence in others?
2. When have you discovered God present in your life?
3. How does your Christmas celebration continue beyond the day and season of Christmas?
4. How can you find God present in this new year?
5. How can you "give back the song" of God's love?

Pray with me

Holy One, be born in us today. Quiet our fears and give us peace. Bless us with your grace. Renew and heal us. Guide us to find new life in you. Help us to receive every gift you offer; let us share your love.

Eleven

Peace on earth

For [Christ Jesus] is our peace; in his flesh he has made both groups into one and has broken down the dividing wall, that is, the hostility between us. (Ephesians 2:14)

At the birth of Jesus the herald angel and a multitude of the heavenly host proclaimed glory to God and peace, goodwill among people (Luke 2:13–14). Jesus the Messiah was the fulfillment of Isaiah's prophecy of a child born to us, a son given to us, with authority resting on his shoulders. He is the Prince of Peace, bringing a promise of endless peace to be upheld with justice and righteousness forever (Isa. 9:6–7). Isaiah also foresaw a time "in days to come" when "the mountain of the Lord's house shall be established as the highest of the mountains" and many peoples "shall beat their swords into plowshares, and their spears into pruning hooks; nation shall not lift up sword against nation, neither shall they learn war any more" (Isa. 2:2, 4). At the Sermon on the Mount, Jesus said "blessed are the peacemakers, for they shall be called children of God" (Matt. 4:9).

And yet, the coming of Jesus was anything but peaceful in a conventional sense. King Herod killed all the male children two and under who

112   Joy to the World!

were in and around Bethlehem in an attempt to protect his crown from
the young child Jesus, born king of the Jews (Matt. 2). Jesus himself died
on a cross, and many of his closest followers died violent deaths (Stephen,
James, Peter, Andrew, and many others). William Alexander Percy states
in his beautiful hymn text "They Cast Their Nets in Galilee" (Hymn 661,
v. 4) that "the peace of God, it is no peace, but strife closed in the sod."

Peace has many meanings. It can mean the absence of war or fighting.
It can signify the end of active conflict or a war. But a truly peaceful reconciliation of enemies may require much more than the end of fighting.
In fact, reconciling or making peace with those who hurt us may seem
unlikely and even suspect. But there can be times when God's presence
makes possible a reconciliation that seemed impossible.

Reconciliation goes deeply to the heart of peace that Christ brings us,
the "heavenly peace" of the sleeping baby Jesus in Joseph Mohr's "Silent
night" (Hymn 111). St. Paul says to the conflicted Ephesian Christians that
Christ Jesus is our peace who breaks down the dividing wall of opposition
and hostility. He reminds us that we are members of the one body of Christ
that includes those who are like us in background and perspective and
those who are not like us. We share a Communion of love with them all.

As we discover God's love in this season of Christmas we may find
ourselves able to forgive. We can let go of old grudges and hurt. We can
refuse to continue old fights. We can find peace as we seek reconciliation,
even if others are not yet ready for it. God's love helps us reach across broken places of estrangement, disappointment, and blame. We can take the
first steps for peace.

Questions to ponder

1. How do you experience the peace of God this Christmas?
2. How can you seek peace on earth with others?
3. Do you need to offer or receive forgiveness?
4. When have you experienced reconciliation?
5. What steps can you take for peace today?

Pray with me

Lord God, Prince of Peace, blessed and holy one, draw us together in your love. Let us end the hostility that separates us from others. Help us find ways to know healing in ourselves and our relationships. Help us to forgive and be forgiven. Guide us to respect others and know them better. Help us to let go of stubbornness, resentment, and the need to put ourselves first. Guide us to remove the dividing walls that separate us from you and each other. Let us find reconciliation whenever possible. Give us your peace.

Twelve

The power of humility

Do nothing from selfish ambition or conceit, but in humility regard others as better than yourselves. Let each of you look not to your own interests, but to the interests of others. Let the same mind be in you that was in Christ Jesus, who, though he was in the form of God, did not regard equality with God as something to be exploited, but emptied himself, taking the form of a slave, being born in human likeness. (Phil. 2:3–7)

Jesus is the divine and human embodiment of humility. The Son of Man had no place to lay his head (Matt. 8:20). When he fasted in the wilderness for forty days and was tempted by the devil, he refused to let his need become the center of his focus or an idol to be worshiped (Luke 4:1–4). Jesus was not self-centered. He had no office or official role. He did not seek worldly advancement or an increase of power. On one occasion the people saw the signs he had done and they were about to "take him by force to make him king, but he withdrew again to the mountain by himself" (John 6:14–16). His kingdom was "not from this world" (John 18:36). He was humble.

We also see Christlike humility in St. Francis of Assisi. He also was not self-centered, not seeking power or advancement in the world. A prayer

The power of humility

attributed to St. Francis gives practical advice for humility and daily living as instruments of God's peace: "Grant that we may not so much seek to be consoled as to console; to be understood as to understand; to be loved as to love. For it is in giving that we receive; it is in pardoning that we are pardoned; and it is in dying that we are born to eternal life" (BCP, 833).

Humility is at the heart of God's activity in the birth of Jesus. St. Athanasius states that God becomes human so we can share the divine life. In Jesus we see God self-emptied (Greek, *kenosis*). At Jesus' birth God comes to us in the flesh as an equal so we may come to God as equals. God does not look down on us; God does not condescend to us. God embraces us by sharing our mortal and vulnerable life. God becomes human for us and our salvation, and raises our humanity to glory.

God saves us by humility. And the humility of Jesus is real, even by human standards. He is born in a stable and placed in a manger. He will learn his first words from his young mother and her husband, a carpenter. He will be a refugee, and flee with his family to Egypt to escape deadly persecution (Matt. 2:13–15). This life of vulnerability and generous sacrifice begins with Jesus' birth. St. Paul invites us to be of the "same mind" with Christ's humility and look beyond our own concerns and positions to the needs of others. We can embrace God fully as we empty ourselves generously. We celebrate a very humble and vulnerable beginning when we celebrate Christmas.

Questions to ponder

1. Does anxious self-concern get in the way
of your love for God and others?
2. Does pride prevent you from forgiving
others or accepting their forgiveness?
3. What helps you to see the needs of others around
you and remember God's presence?
4. How may we empty ourselves and approach each day with humility?

Pray with me

Blessed are you, Holy One, creator and redeemer; you embrace us and the life we live. Jesus, Lord of life, fully divine and fully human, you empty yourself in perfect love; you raise us to divine life and salvation, you surround us with love that unites us with you and each other. We know ourselves most fully in you, dear Lord, and know your love best when we share it freely. We know your generosity when we give ourselves away. We know your forgiveness when we forgive others in your love. Let us find our help in you.

Thirteen

Waters of abundance

Ho, everyone who thirsts, come to the waters; and you that have no money, come, buy and eat! Come, buy wine and milk without money and without price. Why do you spend your money for that which is not bread, and your labor for that which does not satisfy? Listen carefully to me, and eat what is good, and delight yourselves in rich food. Incline your ear, and come to me; listen, so that you may live. I will make with you an everlasting covenant, my steadfast, sure love for David. See, I made him a witness to the peoples, a leader and commander for the peoples. (Isa. 55:1–4)

The waters of God are abundant and quench our thirst. The food of God is plentiful and satisfies every hunger. The grace of God is freely offered; there is enough for all. The love of God surrounds us. We know God's love even more deeply as we share it abundantly.

Sometimes it is easy to fall into a perspective of scarcity. Fear, anxiety, or insecurity can be at the heart of it. What if there is not enough? What if something goes wrong? However much we have may seem to be not enough, leaving us on shaky ground. A scarcity perspective can make us stingy, even tightfisted. We may believe that any gift to another will somehow diminish us: we may fear it will be a zero-sum game, that their gain will be our loss.

A perspective of abundance leads more easily to generosity. There is plenty to share; we have enough. At times we may be amazed to discover that in giving freely we have more to give. Instead of being diminished by what we gave, our generosity is renewed and we find even more to offer in many ways. We are enriched by what we gave, though perhaps in ways that differ from our original gift. We may have more to share than we ever imagined.

Generosity works for the one who gives and the one who receives. We are never alone in situations of giving; our most generous Lord is with us in the moment, and grace is widely shared. God's abundant generosity is known in our generosity. God's abundant forgiveness is known in our forgiveness. God's abundant love is known when we share love with an open heart.

Questions to ponder

1. Have you held back from sharing with others because of worries about scarcity?
2. When have you enjoyed a feeling of abundance?
3. Does your sense of God's presence strengthen a perspective of abundance for you?
4. Have you felt God's generosity active in your own generosity? Have you felt God's forgiveness active in your own forgiveness of others and yourself? Have you felt God's love active in your love for others and yourself?

Pray with me

Holy God, Lord of abundant love, generous giver of life and light for our souls, you bless us with healing, mercy, forgiveness, strength, mission, and inspiration. You fill us with good things; our hearts overflow with the fullness and power of your grace. Move us to share the gifts you offer through us. Let us give ourselves in love for you. Help us to live and give and love abundantly.

Fourteen

In the beginning

In the beginning was the Word, and the Word was with God, and the Word was God. He was in the beginning with God. All things came into being through him, and without him not one thing came into being. What has come into being in him was life, and the life was the light of all people. The light shines in the darkness, and the darkness did not overcome it. (John 1:1–5)

The truth can overwhelm. God the infinite creator of all and everything has come to share life with *us* forever. God is life and light for us; without God we are in darkness and chaos. The light of Christ is not mere illumination but essential and vibrant life. In Christ "we live and move and have our being" (Acts 17:28). In Christ "all things in heaven and on earth were created"; Christ "himself is before all things, and in him all things hold together" (Col. 1:16–17).

The light of Christ was with us in the stable where he was born, and the light of Christ is with us now. A glance at the daily news may convince us we live in dark and dangerous times, but the light shines in the darkness and is not overcome by it. The good news of Jesus' birth is meant to be shared, especially in this beautiful season. Sadly, this can be a dark time for some, a "blue Christmas." Whatever our mood, there is a place for us with Christ. His love surrounds us. As Christ's disciples we will know the truth and the truth will make us free (John 8:31-32). Christ, the light of the world, invites us to share with others the life and love we have received. We know the light of Christ best when we share it. We can reflect a life of hope that shines to overcome darkness. We may brighten things for someone else. Christ is our guide; Christ is our way.

Questions to ponder

1. Have you discovered light in a time of darkness?
2. Have you shared hope in a time of need?
*3. Have you been encouraged in a significant way
by something another person did or said?*
4. Has faith made a difference for you in a time of loss or confusion?

Pray with me

Dear Lord, bring light to our darkness; let your hope scatter our despair. Illumine our minds and warm our hearts. Guide us through our confusion and pain. Help us to follow you; move us to generosity. Let us clearly see the beauty of your love surrounding us. Draw us together in you.

Fifteen

Love first

If I speak in the tongues of mortals and of angels, but do not have love, I am a noisy gong or a clanging cymbal. . . . Love is patient; love is kind; love is not envious or boastful or arrogant or rude. It does not insist on its own way; it is not irritable or resentful; it does not rejoice in wrongdoing, but rejoices in the truth. It bears all things, believes all things, hopes all things, endures all things. Love never ends. (1 Cor. 13:1, 4–8)

A friend of mine visited an Episcopal church for the first time. The service was wonderful. He loved the liturgy. The sermon was inspiring. He was truly impressed. Then he went to coffee hour and stood alone while sipping his coffee. There were lots of other people at coffee hour, greeting their friends, talking together, catching up, but no one reached out to him. So he thought maybe he caught them on a bad day. And so, he went back again.

Like before, he was moved by the beautiful service and the excellent sermon. And again he went to coffee hour. But, once again no one noticed him, and everyone seemed to stay with the people they already knew. It was some years before he found his way back to another Episcopal parish.

Love first

Love is not just a warm feeling. Love is a choice, a commitment to a way of life that lives, gives, shares, welcomes, includes, and advocates. Love "has a look to it," as Rev. Debra Trakel has observed in sermons at St. James in Milwaukee. We are called to follow a way of love in our lives, bringing love to family, friends, people we know, and those we do not yet know. Even our enemies. Love is a way of living that reaches out and offers instead of building walls or isolating. The way of love provides the alternative to putting ourselves first or viewing relationships in merely transactional terms of what the other may do for us. In the second century, Tertullian described a distinctive way to identify Christians: "See how they love one another."

Love takes many shapes, loving all kinds of people in diverse situations. It is more than just loving the people who love us. Jesus asks, "What credit is that to you?" (Luke 6:32) We are called to love strangers, people who may be very different from us, those who try our patience, and enemies (Matt. 5:44). Our loving generosity and kindness extends to those in need who cannot pay us back, including those who are poor or disabled (Luke 14:14). Sharing love encourages love, even in times of difficulty. As St. John of the Cross says, "where there is no love, put love and you will draw out love." Loved by God, we pay forward the gifts of love we receive.

The way of love must be *lived*. Christ calls us to actual generosity, not just an appreciation of the concept of generosity. Christ calls us to actual forgiveness of those who hurt us and to actually forgive ourselves, our own failings—not just an abstract endorsement of forgiveness in principle. Christ calls us to love one another as we are loved by God. This is real love that can be seen and felt, love that makes a difference. Love may take the shape of giving the other what they most need—not necessarily what we are most eager to offer.

The way of love may involve us in reaching out to others who seem difficult to understand and love. And yet we may be surprised to find much in common with the stranger who crosses our path or enters our community. We may find the way of love easier to live if we set aside stereotypes, biases, and fixed expectations concerning others. We may discover love grows as we share it. We may find common ground with another when there seemed to be none. Even old conflicts and hurts can be reconciled when we respond with love and sincere concern for the other.

Sometimes love can be expressed in the simplest of ways, without a lot of fanfare or attention-seeking. My friend visiting the church might have felt a sense of loving welcome into a community with a heart if only someone had noticed him, made him feel welcome, asked about him, invited him to return.

Questions to ponder

1. *Have you ever felt left out or unseen by others? Have you been surprised by love?*
2. *Have you been able to express love for others in ways you did not expect?*
3. *Has loving others helped you to see them differently?*
4. *Has love changed your behavior with others?*
5. *Has loving others helped you to know God's love?*

Pray with me

Lord of our hearts, God of love, help us to give and forgive generously. Walk with us in the way of love and inspire us to offer ourselves in your name. Let your love for each person and all creation be visible in us. Awaken hope, lift our hearts; open our eyes to see your love at work in our lives and in our world. Draw us together in your love; help us to share it!

Sixteen

God's comfort

And I will turn all my mountains into a road, and my highways shall be raised up. Lo, these shall come from far away, and lo, these from the north and from the west, and from the land of Syene. Sing for joy, O heavens, and exult, O earth; break forth, O mountains, into singing! For the Lord has comforted his people, and will have compassion on his suffering ones. (Isa. 49:11–13)

God's comfort is not just to make us cozy. Comfort literally means "with strength" or to strengthen greatly (Latin, *confortare*). God will not leave us comfortless. God comes to us, showing love, revealing love, drawing out love in us, inviting us to share light in a world that can be dark. In Eucharistic Prayer C we pray to God: "Deliver us from the presumption of coming to this Table for solace only, and not for strength; for pardon only, and not for renewal" (BCP, 372). By the grace of God we are strengthened to step out of our comfort zone to live fully, with generosity, courage, and love.

God draws us together in love from many diverse places and perspectives, from near and far and all directions. The wise men came from the

East to Jerusalem to find the newborn Jesus (Matt. 2:1–2). After seeing Jesus, Simeon praised God because he had seen the salvation of God, "a light for revelation to the Gentiles and for glory to your people Israel" (Luke 2:25–32). Jesus announces "the hour has come for the Son of Man to be glorified" after Greeks arrive and tell Philip they wish to see Jesus (John 12:20–23). Our Lord draws together all kinds of people to share divine life, to be at one with God and each other in love. We are stronger together, and we comfort each other.

With God's grace, trusting and confident in divine love for us, we can step forward in ministry, accepting our own risk and vulnerability to help others. Compassion literally means to suffer together or to suffer with (Latin, *compassio*). With God's strengthening we can share others' pain and suffering; we can reach out to serve and heal. We can have strength to face the suffering and pain around us. God strengthens and empowers us to make a difference, overcoming obstacles and discovering hope. God brings strong love and compassion for us; we can share this strength together.

Questions to ponder

1. When have you shared another's suffering, or let another share your pain?
2. How did you find strength at that time? How did you know you were not alone?
3. Did you see new possibilities in the situation?
4. Did you find new hope? How did you know God was with you?

Pray with me

Draw near, dear Lord, and surround us with love. Be with us always. Comfort us when we hurt; strengthen us to overcome fears. Help us to move forward. Let us remove every obstacle that comes between us. Inspire us; walk with us. Guide us to discern your call and serve others. Prepare a place for us with you.

Seventeen

Gleanings of the harvest for the poor and the alien

> *When you reap the harvest of your land, you shall not reap to the very edges of your field, or gather the gleanings of your harvest. You shall not strip your vineyard bare, or gather the fallen grapes of your vineyard; you shall leave them for the poor and the alien: I am the Lord your God.* (Lev. 19:9–10)

Leaving the edges of our field unharvested and unconsumed sets apart some of what we have for others, known or unknown. We leave the edges uncut, available, wild. The gifts we receive are not just for us. This includes spiritual gifts we may share through ministry, as well as the material gifts and advantages we receive. Even if we have "earned" the material gifts through effort, this was possible through everything we have received from beyond ourselves.

When we set aside provision for the poor and alien and outcast, we can perform corporal works of mercy—feeding the hungry, giving drink to the thirsty, giving shelter to the homeless, the refugee, the traveler. We

130   Joy to the World!

serve Christ as we serve the least of his beloved family when they are in need (Matt. 25:31–45).

As we acknowledge our gifts and how much we have received, we may be moved with generosity and concern for the needs of others, strangers, people in need. We may see how we have been helped in surprising ways by people we did not know; and we may seek to help others we do not yet know, taking their needs into account, leaving room for them, including them when possible. We do not have to take everything for ourselves. We can have concern beyond ourselves. We can give as we have received—with unexpected generosity, surprising grace.

I am grateful for the unexpected help of strangers in my life—the stranger who gave me an ice scraper on a cold morning when I struggled to clean my car's windshield; the stranger who stopped to help me when my car was disabled on a country road; the stranger, a cab driver, who found me in a large convention venue and returned the cell phone I dropped in his cab. We can remember how we have been helped and remember the needs of others. We can go out of our way for strangers, help people we do not know, and make room for others in our lives, as our Lord always shares with them a place at His table and in His heart.

Questions to ponder

1. Do you leave room for others? Do you help people you don't know?
2. Do you share some of what you have with others?
3. Have you found God present in people you did not know?
4. Have you been surprised to discover much in common with a person who seemed very different from you?
5. Have you been grateful for the help of a stranger when you were in a new or unexpected situation?

Pray with me

Dear Lord, help us to remember others—the stranger, the poor, and the alien. Let us help the lost and confused, and remember the times when we have needed others' help. Guide our generosity and concern. Help us to give freely, as you constantly provide for us in love. Let us know your mercy in everything we do.

Eighteen

Jesus welcomes the children

People were bringing little children to [Jesus] in order that he might touch them, and the disciples spoke sternly to them. But when Jesus saw this, he was indignant and said to them, "Let the little children come to me; do not stop them, for it is to such as these that the kingdom of God belongs. Truly I tell you, whoever does not receive the kingdom of God as a little child will never enter it." And he took them up in his arms, laid his hands on them, and blessed them. (Mark 10:13–16)

The disciples want to protect Jesus. They know his work is serious, important, and believe that he should not be bothered. In their eyes, it is not the time or place for children. Maybe the kids were playful, noisy, distracting. But Jesus turns the whole situation upside down. He stops the disciples' interference and welcomes the kids. Instead of excluding the children as a possible distraction, he holds them and blesses them. Jesus presents the children as examples of purity and innocence. The kids are not jaded, not hardened or bitter. They are not cynical about motives or

Jesus welcomes the children

outcomes. They can be filled with wonder and awe. They can be amazed; they can believe.

On another occasion Jesus and the disciples were on the way to Capernaum and the disciples argued with each other about who was the greatest. Jesus "took a little child and put it among them; and taking it in his arms, he said to them, 'Whoever welcomes one such child in my name welcomes me, and whoever welcomes me welcomes not me but the one who sent me'" (Mark 9:33–37). Unlike the disciples debating who is the greatest, the kids are not dominated by an agenda or ambition. They are vulnerable because they can love freely, and have not been taught to guard their hearts. And so Jesus wants them protected, kept safe from those who would take advantage of them or abuse them. Jesus warns of woe to the one who would put a stumbling block before "these little ones who believe" (Mark 9:42). Our church today takes many careful steps to provide safe churches for children.

The children's open-heartedness, wonder, willingness to love, eagerness to explore, and play—these are keys to the kingdom of God. Unfortunately, these ways of living seem to be lost or forgotten by many as they grow older. We may seem more like the disciples quarreling over who is the greatest than openhearted and playful children who are amazed by what they see and discover.

In love with Jesus, we can play like children and be open for every blessing. We can romp! We can be amazed and surprised every day. We can be filled with awe; we can believe. We can unbridle our hearts and love generously, playfully, like children—for of such is the kingdom of heaven.

Questions to ponder

1. When have you been filled with awe? When have you felt amazement and wonder?
2. When were you free to explore and discover without self-consciousness or worrying about someone else's opinion?
3. When have you felt safe to let your guard down? Can you play?
4. Can you find God in play? Has God surprised you?

Pray with me

Dear Lord, fill our eyes with wonder and our hearts with love. Let us dance with joy and play in your presence. Amaze us. Show us whatever you want us to see. Help us find new life in you; help us live. Be patient. Laugh with us. Let us sleep in your arms; keep us safe with you. Always be near as we grow in your love.

Nineteen

Jesus' disciples do not fast while he is with them

Now John's disciples and the Pharisees were fasting; and people came and said to him, "Why do John's disciples and the disciples of the Pharisees fast, but your disciples do not fast?" Jesus said to them, "The wedding guests cannot fast while the bridegroom is with them, can they? As long as they have the bridegroom with them, they cannot fast." (Mark 2:18–20)

There was a time in the Episcopal Church when children and others were not admitted to Communion until they were confirmed, and Confirmation for young people was usually around age thirteen or so. And so, as a young child, I would sit in the pew while my family and others went forward to receive Communion. I often noticed that the adults were very serious and solemn when they returned to their seats. They were unsmiling, almost grim. I wondered if the priest gave them something that tasted bad!

While sharing the Eucharist is indeed a solemn occasion, it is also a celebration. We receive God—the flesh and blood of Jesus—within us. We accept him into our lives. We are filled with love. *We rejoice!*

The scribes of the Pharisees criticize Jesus' disciples because they are not fasting. They do not understand that the disciples have much to celebrate. *Jesus is with them.* And he would not let the scribes impose their heavy piety to dampen the celebration. The disciples have new life and a new way forward with Jesus. His way is urgent, demanding, but never glum. We celebrate Christ's life in us with every Eucharist, and in every generous ministry of love in His name. We celebrate our life in Christ, a life that *lives*. The light of Christ dances with us.

Questions to ponder

1. What inspires you?
2. How does Christ bring you new life?
3. Does faith move you to action, awaken your energy, give you purpose and motivation?
4. How do you celebrate God's life with you?
5. Have you invited others to share the celebration?

Pray with me

Holy God of joy and laughter, Lord of songs and gatherings in love for you: Be with us as we celebrate your life in us. Move us with grace that raises hope and brightens despair. Share the love that ends isolation and melts the hardest heart; bring your light into our dark places. Help us welcome those who do not yet know your love. Rejoice with us; dance with us.

Twenty

A fisher of people

As he walked by the Sea of Galilee, he saw two brothers, Simon, who is called Peter, and Andrew his brother, casting a net into the sea—for they were fishermen. And he said to them, "Follow me, and I will make you fish for people." Immediately they left their nets and followed him." As he went from there, he saw two other brothers, James son of Zebedee and his brother John, in the boat with their father Zebedee, mending their nets, and he called them. Immediately they left the boat and their father, and followed him. (Matt. 4:18–22)

Sometimes our Lord calls us into unexpected situations, and we find ourselves stepping into an unknown future as we accept the invitation. It was that way for the fishermen Jesus called to follow him and catch, or "fish," for people, sharing the good news of faith with them. Peter and Andrew, James and John all stepped away from family, friends, their work as fishermen, and their world as they knew it. They left everything behind to follow Jesus. Where were they going? What would they do? What did "fishing for people" even mean to them? What challenges would they face? What were the risks? When would they return? What would come next? There could be no answers for their questions as they left their nets and boats to follow Jesus. They knew they were with him; it was enough to begin their journey and mission. They were on the way.

Dietrich Bonhoeffer describes the disciples' sacrifice in terms of "costly grace." Jesus' invitation was freely offered to the fishermen and simply accepted. But it cost them everything. Bonhoeffer states that costly grace is "the pearl of great price to buy, for which the merchant will sell all his goods. . . . it is the call of Jesus Christ at which the disciple leaves his nets and follows him" (Bonhoeffer, *The Cost of Discipleship*). Stepping into an unknown future can be quite expensive.

We can encounter costly grace in our own lives, and find ourselves stepping into our own unknown futures. The college freshman on the first day of class, the newlyweds walking out the church door together, the newly ordained clergy beginning a new ministry, the parents holding their firstborn child, the worker starting a new job in a new place—where will this new life take them, what will be the demands they face, what will be their sacrifices, what comes next, who will they be? The questions are unanswerable from the beginning, and the answers continue to change. But they can know Christ with them; grace will lead and follow them, and it is enough.

Questions to ponder

1. When have you stepped into an unknown future?
2. What were your biggest challenges? How did you feel?
3. What helped you the most? Were there any surprises?
4. How was God present to you at that time? How did your life change?

Pray with me

Holy Lord of grace and hope, always call us nearer to you. Strengthen our confidence and trust; help us overcome our fears. Draw us forward. Be with us as we step into an unknown future. Let us know you present. Guide us with care. Help us to stand when we fall. Inspire us to use all the gifts you have given us. Move our hearts to share every adventure of life in your love. We will follow you.

Twenty-One

The body of Christ

Now you are the body of Christ and individually members of it. And God has appointed in the church first apostles, second prophets, third teachers; then deeds of power, then gifts of healing, forms of assistance, forms of leadership, various kinds of tongues. Are all apostles? Are all prophets? Are all teachers? Do all work miracles? Do all possess gifts of healing? Do all speak in tongues? Do all interpret? But strive for the greater gifts. (1 Cor. 12:27–31)

What is the best gift you ever gave to someone? Do you give the same gift to everyone, or do you try to choose a gift that is right for each person and situation? One person's treasure might be worthless to someone else. We are different people with different needs, different abilities and challenges, different interests, different gifts to offer, different gifts we need to receive.

God's gifts to us are abundant but distinct and particular to each of us. God's bounty for us is unique, specific—never generic or impersonal. God loves us individually and personally—who we are and can be. We are members of the one body of Christ but never coerced or conformed to a bland sameness. God's love in us and for us is manifested in our many

The body of Christ 141

gifts. The one body of Christ is glorified by the incredible diversity of its countless members, and well served by their myriad gifts. Our various gifts can be complementary, a harmony of different offerings that uphold and strengthen each other.

The gifts we receive may often become the gifts we give. *Do not hide your gifts!* The gifts we receive from God are meant to be put to use and shared. When we have been helped, we can see how important helping is, as we experience ways of helping in our own lives. We engage gifts of leadership when we actually commit to the responsibilities of leadership and work with others in a context of leading. We engage gifts of communication when we reach out to others, sharing ideas, thoughts, feelings, and perspectives to deepen our connections and mutual understanding with them. We do well to consider what the other needs to hear or receive and how they may best receive it. Without engaging others, we neglect our gifts of healing, leadership, communication; without others, our gifts will not be fulfilled in us. Our gifts are meant to be shared.

There was a church that had a beautiful, jeweled chalice. It was very costly. This was not one of the chalices used for Communion services at that church. Those chalices had no jewels, although they were used regularly to share the consecrated wine of the Eucharist. For a time the parish displayed the jeweled chalice in a clear, locked display case in the parish hall, but the chalice was later moved to a safety deposit box. It may have been "safe" there from theft or harm, but it was not used as a chalice. It was not even seen by most people in the church. It did not fulfill its purpose. It was kept in the dark.

Sometimes we may be tempted to play it safe with our greatest gifts. We do not want to risk rejection or failure. We do not want to accept the loss of control and vulnerability that come when other people are involved. But our gifts are at their best when we *use* them; we know our gifts best when we share them with others.

Questions to ponder

1. What are your gifts? Have you hidden your gifts? How can your gifts be used for others?
2. When have you discerned a gift that is yours? Were you surprised?
3. How have you recently shared your gifts? Have you considered new ways to offer your gifts?

Pray with me

Blessed Lord, our generous giver, let your abundance overflow us; fill our hearts and open our hands to share your love with many others. Help us to see you at work in our lives and world. Guide us to use our gifts wisely. Let our gifts always point to you, the giver of everything. May we give generously as we have received.

Twenty-Two

Gifts of mercy

When the Pharisees challenged Jesus's eating with tax collectors and sinners, he said, "Those who are well have no need of a physician, but those who are sick. Go and learn what this means, 'I desire mercy, not sacrifice'" (Matt. 9:11–13).

Mercy is at the heart of the life we share with Christ. We can love as we are loved by our Lord. We can treat others better than they may expect, as Christ provides us loving mercy and forgiveness that is unconditional. Our forgiveness is also to be unconditional and unlimited, "seventy times seven" (Matt. 18:22). We can pay attention to others and respond to their needs instead of hurting or ignoring them. We can be merciful as God is merciful to us.

Mercy takes many shapes. The corporal works of mercy include providing food for the hungry, drink for the thirsty, clothing for those who are not adequately dressed, hospitality for the stranger or traveler, visiting those who are sick or in prison, and burying the dead. The spiritual works of mercy include helping others to convert to faith, instructing others to better understand faith, counseling those with doubts, comforting those

144 Joy to the World!

who are sorrowful, patiently bearing wrongs, forgiving, and praying for the living and the dead. Speaking of giving food to the hungry and drink to the thirsty, welcoming the stranger, clothing the naked, taking care of the sick, and visiting the prisoner, Jesus said, "Truly I tell you, just as you did it to one of the least of these who are members of my family, you did it to me" (Matt. 25:40).

The works of mercy can be a daily reality for us as we give and receive mercifully in all kinds of situations. The works of mercy can be expressed in untraditional ways and unexpected settings. I was glad when a mechanic appeared seemingly out of nowhere to fix my car's engine when I was broken down on an empty highway with no way to call for help. I was stranded, and he was merciful with his skills. I was glad when Victoria—before we were engaged or married—was waiting in my hospital room when I came back from surgery. I was a patient in recovery, and she was merciful by being there.

I was glad near the end of a long, hot half marathon when there was a volunteer with a cup of water to drink. I was thirsty, and the volunteer mercifully offered me something to quench my thirst. Victoria and I were unsure what to do during an ice storm when our house was dark and cold because we lost power for five days. All the local hotels were full. But we were glad when a friend mercifully offered us a place to stay in a warm house. I was glad at a time of significant loss when there was a counselor to talk through the experience with me and offer consolation, encouragement, and insights. It was a work of mercy that made a difference.

Every day we can share gifts like these with mercy. These merciful gifts solve a problem, respond to a need, and draw us closer to each other and our Lord who is at the heart of all we share.

Questions to ponder

1. When have you given and when have you received gifts of mercy?
2. What difference did these gifts make for you and others who shared this experience with you?
3. How did your life and the lives of others change by sharing gifts of mercy?

Pray with me

Gracious Lord, we thank you for your loving mercy and generosity for us in all our days. Help us to be merciful to others in need. Move our compassion. Open our hearts to give and receive forgiveness. Guide us to respond to others' needs. Let us know your love in the love we share. Help us to let go of prejudice, bias, and every obstacle to loving as we are loved by you. Let us be merciful as you are merciful with us.

Twenty-Three

Never forgotten

Can a woman forget her nursing child, or show no compassion for the child of her womb? Even these may forget, yet I will not forget you. See, I have inscribed you on the palms of my hands. . . . (Isa. 49:15–16)

Jesus is God's ultimate gift of love to us and all creation. Instead of being distantly superior to us and remote from the conflicts of our daily life, Christ shares our vulnerability, our hunger and thirst, our pain, our mortality. St. Paul states that Christ was "in the form of God" but "did not regard equality with God as something to be exploited, but emptied himself, taking the form of a slave, being born in human likeness" (Phil. 2:5–7).

In Christ, God self-empties much that is transcendently divine. God is everywhere, omnipresent, but Jesus is at one place at a time. If Jesus is in Jerusalem, he is not in Bethlehem. He travels from place to place with his disciples and followers. God is immortal and timeless, but Jesus ages, and he dies. Jesus is hungry when he fasts; he bleeds when cut; he thirsts on the cross. God is all knowing, omniscient, but Jesus admits he does not know the day or hour of the Son's final coming in power and glory—only God the Father knows when it will be (Matt. 24:36). All these self-emptying sacrifices are made for love as Jesus, the eternal Son of God, fully shares our humanity. God becomes human so humanity can share the divine life (Athanasius, *On the Incarnation*). Jesus, the "pioneer and perfecter of our faith" (Heb. 12:2), opens the way for our salvation. Following the way of our Lord will also involve us in generous sacrifices, our own self-emptying in love. Jesus states "those who lose their life for my sake will find it" (Matt. 16:25).

Christ who throws open the path of completion in God for humanity and all creation is also our Lord who loves each of us personally and fully. Jesus, the Good Shepherd, calls each of his sheep by name and lays down his life for the sheep (John 10:3, 11). Jesus also states that a shepherd with a hundred sheep will leave the ninety-nine and search for just one sheep that has gone astray. He rejoices greatly over the one sheep if he finds it, more than over the ninety-nine who did not go astray (Matt. 18:12–13).

Jesus remembers us, seeks us constantly, guides us when lost or confused, draws us home. He loves each of us that much! Even the hairs of our head are numbered (Luke 12:7). Our Lord knows us that well, and does not forget us. We are inscribed by name in the mind and heart of God.

Questions to ponder

1. *When has love caused you to make an important sacrifice?*
2. *What did this sacrifice make possible for you and others?*
3. *How did this sacrifice change your life?*
4. *When have you felt personally known by God?*

Pray with me

Lord God, creator of heaven and earth and all that is, help us to share the generosity of your love. Guide us to make good choices and be ready to give ourselves when needed. Strengthen us for the sacrifices we must face. Draw near to each of us and help us to know you present. Walk with us, always be with us; let us make our home with you.

Twenty-Four

A new heaven and a new earth

Then I saw a new heaven and a new earth; for the first heaven and the first earth had passed away, and the sea was no more. And I saw the holy city, the new Jerusalem, coming down out of heaven from God, prepared as a bride adorned for her husband. And I heard a loud voice from the throne saying, "See, the home of God is among mortals. He will dwell with them; they will be his peoples, and God himself will be with them; he will wipe away every tear from their eyes. Death will be no more; mourning and crying and pain will be no more, for the first things have passed away." (Rev. 21:1–4)

Diplomacy has been described as the "art of the possible." Sometimes there are diplomatic breakthroughs—prisoners are exchanged, conflicts are ended or paused, peace is restored, agreements are reached when this seemed impossible.

Living Christian faith can also be described as "the art of the possible." In faith, in Christ, we may need to reconsider what is or is not possible.

150 Joy to the World!

William Stringfellow, a lay Episcopal theologian, was a great fan of the circus as "a parable of the eschaton" where performers seemed to move the boundaries between possible and impossible—walking tightropes, swinging on trapezes, taming lions, defying death in amazing ways. Stringfellow explains that "in the circus, humans are represented as freed from consignment to death. . . . The circus performer is the image of the eschatological person—emancipated from frailty and inhibition, exhilarant, militant, transcendent over death—neither confined nor conformed by the fear of death anymore" (Stringfellow, *A Simplicity of Faith*). The circus was for Stringfellow an image of the ultimate hope where life is victorious over death and the everyday boundaries and limits of life are broken.

In Christ the apparent limits of humanity and mortality are broken: "Death will be no more." Christ changes everything by coming into the world and into our lives. In Christ there is a new world of possibility for us all. The light of Christ brings a new delineation of what is possible and impossible. Our hope may appear more clearly. This is true relative to issues of life and death, and relative to every other apparent threat or limitation we face. The impossible conflict or hopeless dilemma we face may be seen by us with new eyes in the light of Christ. With God, "all things are possible" (Matt. 19:26). Christ is born into our world, sharing life and new vision with us. He wipes away every tear.

> ### Questions to ponder
>
>
>
> *1. Have you ever done things you once considered impossible? Have you ever done things that others said would be impossible for you?*
> *2. Has your perspective on what is possible and impossible for you ever changed? What helped or caused the change?*
> *3. How does faith influence your perspective on what is possible and impossible for you?*
> *4. Have you ever helped another person to do something or be someone they once considered impossible?*

Pray with me

O Lord our creator and savior, open our eyes to see you present in each moment. Awaken our hope when we feel discouraged or frustrated. Remind us that our limits are not your limits. Fill our hearts with the wonder of your amazing love. Let us always find you present with us in times of need and times of joy. Surprise us with your love.

Twenty-Five

The repairer of the breach

Is not this the fast that I choose: to loose the bonds of injustice, to undo the thongs of the yoke, to let the oppressed go free, and to break every yoke? Is it not to share your bread with the hungry, and bring the homeless poor into your house; when you see the naked, to cover them, and not to hide yourself from your own kin? Then your light shall break forth like the dawn, and your healing shall spring up quickly. . . . Your ancient ruins shall be rebuilt; you shall raise up the foundations of many generations; you shall be called the repairer of the breach, the restorer of streets to live in. (Isa. 58:6–8, 12)

Why does God become human? That's what St. Anselm of Canterbury asks in his book of the same name (Anselm, *Why God Became Man* [Latin, *Cur Deus Homo?*]). We may answer Anselm's question with the help of the Nicene Creed: "For us and for our salvation he came down from heaven: by the power of the Holy Spirit he became incarnate from the Virgin Mary, and was made man" (BCP, 358). We may add that Christ's ministry is true to the messianic expectation and anticipates its fulfillment. He is the Expected One who is to make right what is wrong in our world and in our lives so that what is incomplete in us and in our world may be

The repairer of the breach 153

complete in God. This is our salvation and the redemption of all things. Christ is "the Savior and Redeemer of the world" (Eucharistic Prayer B, BCP, 368).

We now live "between the times," between the first advent of the Son and the ultimate fulfillment of Christ in power and glory. Our Lord's ministry on earth is already begun but not yet complete or fulfilled. In the meantime, the work of building Christ's kingdom on earth is ours to share. We pray for the advent of God's kingdom "on earth as in heaven" (The Lord's Prayer, BCP, 97). The coming of God's kingdom on earth happens with and through us by our participation. As we receive divine grace and inspiration, we can engage God's mission on earth with our lives. We can use our gifts on behalf of their giver to reflect Christ's love in the world. We can fight against the bonds of injustice and the yoke of oppression. In the words of St. Mary, we can stand with God who "has cast down the mighty from their thrones, and has lifted up the lowly"; we can share the work of God who "has filled the hungry with good things," and sent the rich away empty (Luke 1:52-53; The Song of Mary, BCP, 92).

In the dawning new light of Christ's coming to this world and to us, we can minister and share his love. We can provide housing for the homeless, clothing for the naked, comfort for the troubled. In Christ, we can proclaim to the poor "the good news of salvation; to prisoners, freedom; to the sorrowful, joy" (Eucharistic Prayer D, BCP, 374). As stated by the prophet Isaiah, we can rebuild the ancient ruins, raise new foundations, welcome the new age of Christ's coming, and repair the breach.

Questions to ponder

1. Have you encountered breaches in your world and in your life?
2. Have you seen breaches in collaboration, cooperation, relationships, love? What have you done to repair these breaches?
3. Have you found help from beyond yourself to repair the breaches?
4. Have you found occasions and ways to fight injustice, to respond to human need with compassion, to protect nature as God's creation, and to seek reconciliation instead of antagonism and estrangement? How?

Pray with me

Holy God, gracious and mighty, bring new light and life to the darkness of our world and our lives. Give us hope for the future. Build your kingdom on earth as in heaven, and let us help. Let us minister and share your justice, compassion, healing, and love. Inspire us; strengthen us for service and help us to use the gifts we have received with your blessing. Let your light break like the dawn in our hearts. Help us to repair the breaches we encounter in our world and our lives. Move us to raise new foundations.

Twenty-Six

The peace of the Lord

How beautiful upon the mountains are the feet of the messenger who announces peace, who brings good news, who announces salvation, who says to Zion, "Your God reigns." Listen! Your sentinels lift up their voices, together they sing for joy; for in plain sight they see the return of the Lord to Zion. Break forth together into singing, you ruins of Jerusalem; for the Lord has comforted his people, he has redeemed Jerusalem. (Isa. 52:7–10)

At Jesus' birth an angel heralded to the shepherds the birth of "a Savior, who is the Messiah, the Lord." And suddenly "there was with the angel a multitude of the heavenly host, praising God and saying: 'Glory to God in the highest heaven, and on earth peace among those whom he favors'" (Luke 2:11, 13–14). The birth of Jesus brings peace to earth. He is the fulfillment of Isaiah's prophecy: "For a child has been born to us, a son given to us; authority rests upon his shoulders; and he is named Wonderful Counselor, Mighty God, Everlasting Father, Prince of Peace" (Isa. 9:6).

In the Sermon on the Mount, Jesus said, "Blessed are the peacemakers, for they will be called children of God" (Matt. 5:9). When the risen Jesus appeared to his disciples on the evening of the day of his resurrection,

156 Joy to the World!

they were hiding behind locked doors in fear. His first words to them were words of peace. Jesus stood among the disciples and said to them: "Peace be with you." He showed them his hands and side, they rejoiced to see him, and again he said to them: "Peace be with you." Jesus breathed on the disciples to give them the Holy Spirit, and commissioned them to forgive sins (John 20:19–23).

Jesus comes to us and enters our world in peace. The peace of Jesus is most especially the presence of our Lord and His love. He seeks to draw us together in love. In him we share the life and unity of God's own life so we all may be one. He invites us to be peacemakers, to overcome hatred with love, to seek reconciliation instead of revenge, to tear down walls of opposition and fear, to find common ground and mutual understanding. Our Lord would be scandalized by the spectacle of Christians hurting other Christians or anyone else in his name. Hatred, division, bias, prejudice—all block the sharing of Jesus' love that is our salvation and our peace.

Jesus' offer of peace to his disciples takes place in the midst of the storm of controversy that brutally ended his mortal life. The threat to his disciples is real; their motivation to hide is understandable. And yet never again do we see the disciples hiding out for fear of anybody after Jesus blesses them with his peace, even though the threats surrounding them are unchanged. The peace Jesus shares with his disciples is the gift of his saving presence. Jesus will be with them; his love will surround them. Sharing the peace of Jesus, the disciples unlock the door and go out into the world with mission to heal, to forgive, and to save in Jesus' name. They will be peacemakers.

We also share the peace of the Lord at every Eucharist when the celebrant says to the people: "The peace of the Lord be always with you." After the people respond in kind, "And also with you," the ministers and people greet each other in the name of the Lord (BCP, 360). They "pass the peace of Christ," celebrating God really present with them in their gathering for Eucharist. The peace of the Lord that surrounds them and draws them together in love will also be with them as they go forth from Holy Communion. The deacon or celebrant may dismiss the gathering with a reminder of what they will continue to share: "Go in peace to love and serve the Lord." We can do our part to share the peace of Christ in the world, the peace of God that "surpasses all understanding" (Phil. 4:7), and make the peaceable kingdom of God a reality on earth as in heaven.

Questions to ponder

1. How have you known the peace of Christ?
How have you known Christ's presence?
2. How have you shared the peace of Christ with others?
3. When have you been a peacemaker?
4. How does a life of peace make a difference for you?

Pray with me

Holy Lord, Prince of Peace, warm our hearts and surround us with your love. Help us to know you present with us; let us welcome others in your name. Let us be peacemakers. Help us listen to everyone, especially those who differ from us. Guide us to seek forgiveness and reconciliation instead of revenge when there has been division, hurt or anger. Help us to live in peace and make peace in your world.

Twenty-Seven

The peaceable kingdom

The wolf shall live with the lamb, the leopard shall lie down with the kid, the calf and the lion and the fatling together, and a little child shall lead them. The cow and the bear shall graze, their young shall lie down together; and the lion shall eat straw like the ox. The nursing child shall play over the hole of the asp, and the weaned child shall put its hand on the adder's den. They will not hurt or destroy on all my holy mountain; for the earth will be full of the knowledge of the Lord as the waters cover the sea. (Isa. 11:6–9)

The peaceable kingdom described by Isaiah is a startling image of natural enemies dwelling happily together on God's holy mountain: wolf and lamb, leopard and kid, calf and lion, venomous snakes, and very young children. And, Isaiah says, "a little child shall lead them." Christ comes into our world and lives as the ultimate expression of God's love for the world, reconciling and redeeming all the apparent opposites and antagonists. Christ comes "for us and for our salvation" (Nicene Creed, BCP, 358), removing, forgiving, and healing the many obstacles we put between ourselves and God, between ourselves and each other.

The peaceable kingdom 159

Christ directs us to love our enemies and not judge them. God's love and blessings are extended to everyone. God "makes his sun rise on the evil and on the good, and sends rain on the righteous and on the unrighteous" (Matt. 5:45). Whatever our failings or shortcomings, we have a place in God's peaceable kingdom if we accept it.

We may find ourselves sharing the peaceable kingdom in Christ for eternity with unexpected and unlikely companions. It is a humbling prospect that gives urgency to sharing God's peaceable kingdom in this world with those who differ from us, even our enemies. We do not want our divisions to impede the unity of that Day, the coming of the Son in power and glory, the completion of all things.

Miroslav Volf tells the story of a time when Karl Barth was asked whether we will one day see our loved ones in heaven. He is reported to have said, "Not only the loved ones!" I expect Barth was smiling when he said it. Christ who shares life eternal with us also shares eternal life with those who dismay us. In "The Final Reconciliation," Volf writes that "the not-loved-ones will have to be transformed into the loved ones and those who do not love will have to begin to do so; enemies will have to become friends." The conclusion is inescapable: Christians "had better learn to love each other now since they will spend eternity together" (Volf, "The Final Reconciliation").

At the conclusion of his "I Have a Dream" speech, Martin Luther King Jr. draws on Isaiah 40:5 (KJV) to eagerly anticipate a time when "the glory of the Lord will be revealed and all flesh shall see it together." This means *everyone*. King offers a vision of the peaceable kingdom "when we allow freedom to ring, when we let it ring from every village and every hamlet, from every state and city, we will be able to speed up that day when *all* of God's children—black men and white men, Jews and Gentiles, Catholics and Protestants—will be able to join hands and to sing in the words of the old Negro spiritual, '*Free at last! Free at last! Thank God Almighty, we are free at last!"* (King, "I Have a Dream," Lincoln Memorial, March on Washington for Jobs and Freedom, Washington, D.C., August 28, 1963).

We can share the peaceable kingdom now with all kinds of people—enemies, strangers, people who differ from us. We can put down the weapons of violence, bias, and prejudice that separate us from others. We can beat our swords into plowshares and our spears into pruning hooks (Isa. 2:4). The community we share now can itself be a "foretaste of the heavenly banquet," a peaceable kingdom where all are included.

Questions to ponder

1. Have you seen occasional glimpses of the peaceable kingdom?
2. Have you helped to build the peaceable kingdom in this world?
3. What needs to change for the peaceable kingdom to be a reality for you?
4. Have you taken steps to reconcile a disagreement or division?
5. Have you made peace in a time of conflict?

Pray with me

Holy God, reconciler of enemies, lover of wounded hearts, draw us together with those we love and those we struggle to love. Guide us to forgive and accept forgiveness, help us to forgive ourselves. May your strong love draw us together despite anything that would tear us apart. May we all be united forever in the peaceable kingdom. Let us share the new Day of your love together.

Epiphany Season

Brightest and Best

Magi

*Sunk in darkness,
far from home;
heavy with treasure,
shivering cold—*

A star appears.

*Jewels and gold
glitter, sumptuous;
the best we had.*

*Satin knees
on coarse ground
for adoration.*

The child's eyes open.

We let ourselves out
into a world
we didn't remember.

Peace is broken—
a cry in the night,
and blood.

Wasted lives left behind:
a new dream
a new life
a new road.

—From *Anglican Theological Review 84:1*,
Robert Boak Slocum

One

Epiphanies

And the Word became flesh and lived among us, and we have seen his glory, the glory as of a father's only son, full of grace and truth. (John 1:14)

An epiphany is a manifestation, a showing, a revelation, a moment of clarity and deep understanding. Many of Jesus' miracles and events of wonder had immediate impact that made a significant difference for the lives of others. Jesus healed many who were sick or impaired. The blind received sight, the deaf received hearing, leprosy was cured, the hemorrhaging woman was healed. He raised Lazarus from the dead and returned him to mortal life. Jesus resolved threatening situations of crisis or great difficulty. He calmed the waters during a windstorm on the lake when he was in a boat with his disciples, and they were afraid. He turned water into wine at a wedding reception and avoided a major embarrassment for the hosts. The risen Jesus showed the fishermen where to cast their net for a huge catch of fish after they had worked all night without catching anything (John 21).

There were also spectacular moments. Jesus was transfigured in glory on the holy mountaintop. He walked on the sea and amazed his disciples who were facing rough waters in the boat. The resurrected Jesus appeared

164 Joy to the World!

to the disciples in the room where they gathered on the day of resurrection and again a week later.

Jesus' epiphanies were helpful, stunning, and memorable for those who witnessed these events. But the epiphanies pointed beyond their immediate benefit or impact to a much greater truth. Jesus' epiphanies showed him to be the Christ, the Lord, the Messiah, the Expected One. The epiphanies were often spectacular, but they were not just spectacles, not just showings of raw divine power because God *can*, not a show of force to frighten and intimidate.

The epiphanies point the witnesses (and us) in the direction of belief in Jesus the Christ. The man who was paralyzed is able to stand and go home after Jesus heals him; the crowds who witness this healing are filled with awe and glorify God (Matt. 9:1–7). When Jesus cures a demoniac who was blind and mute, "All the crowds were amazed and said, 'Can this be the Son of David?'" (Matt. 12:22–23) After Jesus walks on the sea and saves Peter when he tries to walk on the water, the disciples in the boat worship Jesus and say to him, "Truly you are the Son of God" (Matt. 14:22–33). When Jesus calms the windstorm and raging waves on the lake, the disciples were "afraid and amazed, and said to one another, 'Who then is this, that he commands even the winds and the water, and they obey him?'" (Luke 8:22–25) After Jesus heals a person with leprosy, people came to him "from every quarter" (Mark 1:40–45). After a miraculous catch of fish at Jesus' direction, Simon Peter falls down at Jesus' knees and says, "Go away from me, Lord, for I am a sinful man!" (Luke 5:1–8) The centurion who witnesses Jesus' death on the cross says, "Truly this man was God's Son!" (Mark 15:39)

The epiphanies of Jesus manifest his divinity, providing clarity and deep understanding for those who witness and believe in the Christ, our Lord, the Son of God.

Questions to ponder

1. How has God been manifest to you?
2. What has pointed you to see and know God present with you?
3. Have you witnessed the glory of God visible in the world?
4. When have you seen new life in yourself or others?
5. How has God's presence in the world made a difference for you?

Pray with me

Blessed are you, Lord God, creator of life, source of our hope and renewal, reveal your glory, open our eyes to see you present with us. Inspire us and give us strength to follow you, let us share the bright light and peace of your love.

Two

The star at its rising

When the wise men saw that the star had stopped, they were overwhelmed with joy. On entering the house, they saw the child with Mary his mother; and they knelt down and paid him homage. Then, opening their treasure chests, they offered him gifts of gold, frankincense, and myrrh. (Matt. 2:10–12)

The star in the East was an epiphany, a manifestation of who Jesus was and what occurred at his birth. The wise men discerned the significance of the star in the night sky. The star brought them to the child Jesus; it brought them joy. The star brought the wise men an occasion for worship and an opportunity to offer their best gifts. Many others saw the star but missed its meaning. We need to keep our eyes open for epiphanies of God with us. Epiphanies can attract our attention, startle our understanding, move us to action. We may be led forward on unexpected journeys and surprising quests. We may find joy as we discover God with us in so many ways. We may offer our hearts in worship and discover new gifts to present.

With our gifts we offer ourselves in tangible, visible ways. Gifts are in a sense sacramental—outward and visible signs of our inward and spiritual experience of grace. With our gifts we reveal our love, generosity, and compassion or concern for another or others. The gifts we receive can become or shape the gifts we give. We can pay it all forward. If we have received important gifts, we know how much gifts can mean for others to receive. We want others to know they are gifted. Sometimes we know our gifts best when we give them away.

The wise men gave Jesus the best they had, gifts fit for a king. They humbled themselves before him. We may know God's generosity best when our hands are open and we share widely and wildly. We may know God's forgiveness most fully when we forgive others readily. We may know God's love best when our hearts overflow abundantly with love for others.

Questions to ponder

1. How has Christ been manifest in your life?
2. How have you seen Christ present, or been aware of Christ's presence?
3. What signs or reflections of Christ's glory have helped you to follow Christ?
4. Where has Christ led you? How has your life changed in faith?

Pray with me

Blessed are you, Holy One, Jesus Christ, your glory is brilliant, your light is salvation and life. Be known to us in every day. Open our eyes. Strengthen us to offer our gifts and help others to follow you.

Three

The glory of the Lord

Arise, shine, for your light has come, and the glory of the Lord has dawned upon you. For behold, darkness covers the land; deep gloom enshrouds the peoples. But over you the Lord will rise, and his glory will appear upon you. Nations will stream to your light, and kings to the brightness of your dawning. (Isa. 60:1–3; BCP, Canticle 11, 87)

Christ comes into the world to save us, not to punish or overpower us. The light of Christ is with us for our completion, our salvation, the drawing out of our gifts and abilities—not our scolding or humiliation. We could have been made by God to be like puppets or obedient robots. But God invites us to share a relationship of love that saves us. Love must be freely given, never forced or coerced.

Forced obedience, a robotic compliance, would not be the love that God seeks nor the best use of our gifts. In Christ we offer ourselves fully. We engage our autonomy and creativity to the full when embraced by God's love. Austin Farrer describes the power of "double agency," divine and human agency freely working together (Farrer, *The Glass of Vision*).

At the Easter Vigil the Paschal Candle bearing the new fire is brought into the darkened church, a symbol of the light of Christ that illumines the darkness of our world and our hearts. Members of the congregation may then light their candles from the Paschal Candle and the light of Christ spreads through the church (BCP, 285–295). The light grows and is not diminished by being shared, as our love of Christ deepens when we reach out to others in the love of Christ. The light of Christ illumines the darkness and brings peace to conflict, reconciliation to strife, connection to loneliness, hope to despair, forgiveness to guilt, confidence and trust to fear, healing to injury, consolation and comfort to grief and loss.

We are most fully ourselves when we embrace God's life active in us; we are most ourselves when we are most fully *His*. Our Lord calls us friends, and welcomes us to share his life in powerful and vibrant ways. Instead of cowering in fear we stand in faith. We shine with the light of Christ. Arise, shine! Your light has come! (Isaiah 60:1; BCP, Canticle 11, 87)

Questions to ponder

1. How were you drawn to faith? What did you see?
2. Were you in the dark when God found you? Did faith bring light to you?
3. How do you discover God present in your life?
4. Where do you see God's glory?
5. What difference does this make for you?

Pray with me

O Lord, our God, be our light in the darkness. Help us to find our way to you. Lead us through our confusion and fear. May your love dawn in our hearts. Brighten our spirits; awaken hope. Prepare a place for us.

Four

An incredible catch

They went out and got into the boat, but that night they caught nothing. . . . [Jesus] said to them, "Cast the net to the right side of the boat, and you will find some." So they cast it, and now they were not able to haul it in because there were so many fish. . . . Jesus said to them, "Bring some of the fish that you have just caught." So Simon Peter went aboard and hauled the net ashore, full of large fish, a hundred fifty-three of them; and though there were so many, the net was not torn. (John 21:3, 6, 10–11)

Peter and other disciples were fishermen when Jesus called them to follow him and become, instead, fishers of *people* (Matt. 4:19). They did follow Jesus, perhaps for about the next three years. Jesus was their leader. If Jesus went to Capernaum, the disciples went to Capernaum; if Jesus went to Jerusalem, they followed him there. They were his chosen followers.

But Jesus' death on the cross left the disciples leaderless. They rejoiced at the risen Jesus' two appearances in the room where they gathered, but Jesus was no longer with them on a daily basis to provide guidance and direction. Where would they go? What would they do?

Peter went back to what he did for work before he followed Jesus. He knew the job well. He went fishing, followed by the disciples who were with

172   Joy to the World!

him by the Sea of Tiberias. Instead of fishing for people, they were fishing
for fish again. It did not go well at first. They worked all night and caught
nothing. But with Jesus' direction, they caught so many fish they struggled
to haul in the net. Simon Peter was able to bring in the catch—153 large
fish—without tearing the net.

The fishermen were frustrated until they received the blessing of Jesus'
direction, and then their catch was incredible, overwhelming, almost too
much to handle. Jesus' presence and blessing seems to have realigned the
disciples with their true vocation to be fishers of people. Never again do we
see the disciples returning to the fishing business. They become Christian
leaders; they share the Good News of salvation in Christ; they engage the
apostolic ministry Jesus gave them.

St. Jerome believed the number of large fish in the catch (153) represented
the universality of the disciples' calling because the fish biologists of the
day believed there were 153 different kinds of fish. Jerome may have been
wrong about the fish biology of the New Testament era, but the numbering
of the fish (an unusually specific detail in this narrative) seems to point to
the universal breadth and diversity of the disciples' calling (and ours) to be
wide-ranging and inclusive fishers of people. Raymond Brown states "the
catch becomes symbolic of missionary success in bringing people into the
one community of Christ" (Brown, *An Introduction to the New Testament*).
Our own missionary "fishing" may draw to faith a "catch" of all kinds and
descriptions of people. "The net of God's love travels gently through the
waters and picks up many unlikely and unusual fish" (Slocum, "A Heart
for the Future"). Let down the nets!

Questions to ponder

1. Have you felt lost with no way forward?
2. Were you tempted to go backwards to an earlier way of life?
3. Has God moved you toward your best life when you were faltering?
4. Have you been surprised by the opportunities available to you as you seek your best direction?

Pray with me

Holy God, Lord of life, lover of souls, come quickly to help us when we falter. Treat us patiently when we fall back; always guide us forward to find ourselves in you. Help us to see you present. Give us clarity, strength, and courage to claim every gift you offer us. Let us share the abundant love we constantly receive from you.

Five

A great light in the darkness

The people who walked in darkness have seen a great light; those who lived in a land of deep darkness—on them light has shined. You have multiplied the nation, you have increased its joy; they rejoice before you as with joy at the harvest, as people exult when dividing plunder. For the yoke of their burden, and the bar across their shoulders, the rod of their oppressor, you have broken as on the day of Midian. (Isa. 9:2–4)

Walking after sunset and before "last light" can be challenging; walking in total darkness can be impossible. You cannot see where you are going. You lose your sense of direction and cannot retrace your steps. You may fall in a ditch or walk into a door.

I was once spending the night with friends in a house I thought I knew well. I was walking from one room to another. The lights were out and everyone else was asleep. I did not want to disturb them by turning on any lights. *I know my way,* I thought confidently to myself. The house was really dark, and about halfway across the second room, I had lost my

A great light in the darkness 175

sense of direction. *Well,* I thought, *I can return to where I started.* But the room was dark all around and I had no sense of forward or backward. I was stuck in the dark. With some embarrassment I called to my friend who turned on a light and "rescued" me.

Sometimes it is hard for us to discover the way forward. We may find ourselves in situations that leave us confused, disoriented, or conflicted. That can be our wilderness, our place where we feel lost and abandoned. Without light we have no vision, our eyes are useless. We can also be without vision, no sense of direction, and hopeless without the light of Christ. We stumble along lost in our own darkness. We feel helpless in isolation.

If we find ourselves lost in the dark, we can ask for help. God can do a new thing in us. The situation may begin to clear in a moment. Someone may say what we most need to hear. A door that was long closed may begin to open. God may surprise us by the very nearness of love in the midst of our crisis. The whisper and hand of God's presence may take many forms, opening unexpected possibilities and solutions. We may discover rivers in the desert, water for our thirst, guidance for our searching. The bright glory of God comes to us—light to scatter the darkness, hope to overcome despair, meaning and direction instead of confusion.

Questions to ponder

1. Have you ever been lost in darkness? Have you been surprised to discover what you need the most?
2. Were you literally unable to see, or was the difficulty of your darkness all too clear and visible for you?
3. Did you feel trapped, alone, helpless? Did you find a new direction forward?
4. How does light reach you when things seem dark? What makes the difference for you now?
5. Where do you find the light of Christ? Do you find Christ's light reflected in others? How about in you?

Pray with me

Holy God, dear Lord, our hope and inspiration, come quickly to help us. Find us when we are lost; be with us. Guide us to new possibilities when we despair. Let us find strength in you when we fear. Help us to discover a better way; guide us on our path. Let us begin an adventure of faith. Surprise us with the power of your love. Bring light in our darkness, water in the desert. Brighten our path and guide us to you.

Six

The salt of the earth

"You are the salt of the earth; but if salt has lost its taste, how can its saltiness be restored? It is no longer good for anything, but is thrown out and trampled under foot. You are the light of the world. A city built on a hill cannot be hid. No one after lighting a lamp puts it under the bushel basket, but on the lampstand, and it gives light to all in the house. In the same way, let your light shine before others, so that they may see your good works and give glory to your Father in heaven." (Matt. 5:13–16)

Without seasoning, and especially without salt, food can taste pretty bland. Seasoning can give a distinctive taste to our meal. Our faith makes life distinctive in ways that can be shared, but some Christians are shy and reluctant to claim their faith or suggest that faith has something to offer others. Perhaps they do not want to take the risk of vulnerability that comes with sharing anything that touches their heart, or maybe they hesitate to discuss anything personal with someone they do not know well. It is easy to take for granted or forget every gift we receive from God in faith. We may become lukewarm in our faith, neither hot nor cold. The Book of Revelation (3:16) warns sharply against this approach to the Christian life. We can move beyond a bland, lukewarm, hidden faith to living in a way that reflects the light of Christ in us. We can share the life and love we have received in faith.

I once saw a poster with instructions for using the Heimlich maneuver to help a person who is choking by dislodging a blockage. At the end of the instructions the poster urged: "Do this to make a difference!" There should be nothing half-hearted about saving a life! In a similar way, there should be nothing half-hearted in our living and sharing faith, or our ministry for others.

The manifestations of epiphany continue today and in our own lives. The light of Christ is no secret. God's love can be seen in us despite our imperfections. We are called to be transparent to God with us; we can make Christ's love visible. Each of us may be the best translation of the Gospel that some people will ever encounter.

In Christ we are to be the salt of the earth, the light of the world. *No hiding!* By our actions and words we reflect the light of God's glory. Transformative faith is best known when seen and lived. *Let your light shine!*

Questions to ponder

1. How do you show the light in you?
2. How do you express most fully who you are?
3. How does faith make a difference in your life?
4. Have you recognized Christ's presence in the lives of others?
5. How can the love of Christ be seen in your life? How can your light shine before others?

Pray with me

Loving God, give us strength and courage to share your light in the world. Let us claim you gladly and without fear. Help us to be truly yours and reveal your glory in the world as we disclose our true selves. Let our lives point to you. May your light shine in us.

Seven

A covenant with God

Thus says the Lord: In a time of favor I have answered you, on a day of salvation I have helped you; I have kept you and given you as a covenant to the people, to establish the land, to apportion the desolate heritages; saying to the prisoners, "Come out," to those who are in darkness, "Show yourselves." (Isa. 49:8–9)

God makes covenants with us. Contracts may be broken when one of the parties to the contract fails to perform, but covenants cannot be broken. Covenants are unconditional for both parties. That is good news for us. We may fall short at times, but God remains with us—undaunted, persistent, loving, available in relationship, always honoring His covenant with us.

For our part, living a covenant with others usually requires forgiveness. Human covenants are challenging because we are imperfect. The "Celebration and Blessing of a Marriage" includes a prayer for the newly married couple: "Grant them grace, when they hurt each other, to recognize and acknowledge their fault, and to seek each other's forgiveness and yours" (BCP, 429). Despite the best intentions and the strongest commitment, the couple will from time to time make mistakes, do or say things that hurt each other. They are not perfect people and they will not be perfect spouses. But each can seek and accept the other's forgiveness, moving forward in their life together when they hurt each other.

How many times will we need to be forgiven in our performance of a covenant? How many times must we forgive another's performance in a covenant? How many times must we forgive ourselves in the same covenant? Countless times, Jesus says, seventy times seven (Matt. 18:22), an expression for times of forgiveness beyond counting.

God holds on to us even when we let go. God with us empowers us, upholding us with promises that will be fulfilled. Trusting in God, we can have confidence to offer ourselves fully and engage real challenges. We can face opposition without being overwhelmed. We are not alone. We move forward out of darkness into light. We can face our own imperfections and those of others. We can do something about the obstacles that hold us back. We can show ourselves, unafraid, transparent to the light in us.

Questions to ponder

1. What are the major obstacles you have faced?
2. What obstacles are you facing now?
3. When have you needed another's forgiveness? When have you needed to forgive another?
4. What helps you the most? What gives you hope?
5. How do you find God present in times of difficulty? How does the Lord comfort you and give you strength?

Pray with me

God of glory, Lord of hope, be near as we struggle with our challenges, obstacles, and confusion. Show us your mercy and love. Comfort us when we hurt. Sustain us with your strength. Always stand with us. Raise us when we fall. Guide us when we are lost. Inspire us; let us share your love in the world.

Eight

The creation

In the beginning when God created the heavens and the earth, the earth was a formless void and darkness covered the face of the deep, while a wind from God swept over the face of the waters. Then God said, "Let there be light"; and there was light. And God saw that the light was good; and God separated the light from the darkness. God called the light Day, and the darkness he called Night. And there was evening and there was morning, the first day. (Gen. 1:1–5)

Creation continues. God, the originator of all, is creatively and constantly with us. God the creator in the beginning is active with us in each new beginning and all that follows. God continues to move us toward completion in divine love. All goes out from God; all returns to God (Latin, *exitus et reditus*). Human completion in God is visible in Jesus but not yet completed in us. Even now we live in the promise of a wholeness and oneness with God that we may only glimpse "through a glass, darkly" in the present, "but then face to face," when we share the ultimate completion of God's life and love (1 Cor. 13:12 KJV).

Meanwhile, between the times of Christ's first coming and the completion and fulfillment of all in Christ, creation continues. God who brings

184 Joy to the World!

light for the first day also shares light for us now in ways we can see and in ways we cannot see. God is with us, alive and active, healing, inspiring, moving us to accept the grace and fulfill the promise that saves us. God creates in us a new heart and draws us to him, sharing divine life and love. Creation continues in us. Christ is the promise, the way, the power of salvation, the end and fulfillment of our creation.

God the creator is creatively active in each of us. The grace of God always comes first. But we must accept and engage the gift of grace that invites us to continue our own creative process leading to completion in God. Like Mary, we must say the *yes* of faith to proceed with God's surprising invitation. Like the fishermen Peter and Andrew, James and John, we must respond to Jesus who beckons us to a new way of life. They got out of their boats, left their fishing nets behind, and stepped into an unknown future.

At times our next steps may become more challenging as we go. Some time after Peter's first steps in faith, Jesus invites him to walk on water. Peter is able to take miraculous first steps toward Jesus who is on the water, but Peter is soon overcome by fear and doubt. He begins to sink and is rescued by Jesus (Matt. 14:25–33). Dietrich Bonhoeffer explains that "Christ must first call [Peter], for the step can only be taken at his word. This call is his grace, which calls him out of death into the new life of obedience" (Bonhoeffer, *The Cost of Discipleship*).

Even though Peter can only make a few incredible steps on the water, he continues to grow in grace as he once again is able to get out of a boat and respond in faith to Jesus' invitation for steps into the unknown. We also can participate in an ongoing process of accepting creative grace that renews us, heals us, challenges us, and saves us with daily steps into new life.

Questions to ponder

1. What has God created in you? What has changed for you in responding to God's love?
2. What has God inspired you to create? What new or unexpected steps have you taken in faith?
3. In your experience does new creation happen all at once or over a period of time?
4. When has new creation made a difference for you? How do you begin a new day in faith?
5. Has God helped you to make a new beginning? What are the next steps to move forward?

Pray with me

Holy God, loving creator, source of light and life, you bring each new day and every opportunity to love and serve. Open our eyes so we can see you active in our world and our lives. Draw out our best. Guide us always to take the next steps that lead us closer to you. Help us to release fears and anxious self-concern. Surprise us with new ways to share an adventure of faith. Be light in our darkness. Let this new day sparkle in our hearts with your love.

Nine

The true focus

[John] proclaimed, "The one who is more powerful than I is coming after me; I am not worthy to stoop down and untie the thong of his sandals. I have baptized you with water; but he will baptize you with the Holy Spirit." (Mark 1:7–8)

John the Baptist was the voice crying in the wilderness to prepare the way of the Lord and make the paths straight. John went throughout the regions of the River Jordan to proclaim a baptism of repentance, and the crowds came to him. The people wondered whether he was the expected Messiah, but he quickly pointed away from himself to the one who was coming, the one who would baptize with the Holy Spirit and fire (Luke 3).

I remember a retreat I attended where the leader of the retreat made a point of sitting to the side at the front of the chapel where we met. He said, "Do not look at me; look at the cross on the altar" to focus. What we were doing there was not about him, the retreat leader. John was also clear that he was not to be the center of attention. John was with two of his own disciples when he pointed to Jesus and said, "Look, here is the Lamb of

God!"; they heard John and followed Jesus (John 1:35–36). Many images of John depict him pointing to Jesus, the expected one, the Messiah. John said relative to Jesus, "He must increase, but I must decrease" (John 3:30). John was a humble prophet.

Jesus the eternal Son of God is manifested not only by his own works but also by the witness of those who point to him in faith. "Do not look at me," John says, "Look at him." John models our own discipleship and Christian witness. Our expressions of faith—every service, works of mercy, generous giving, acts of devotion—all point beyond ourselves and our actions. The best of what we do points to our Lord and reflects his love, making him visible and better known. That is our epiphany.

Questions to ponder

1. Have there been times when you pointed beyond yourself to Christ?
2. Have others served as pointers to Christ for you? Have you been able to see Christ present in others?
3. Have you witnessed epiphanies in your own life or in the lives of others? Have you discovered God present in a time of need?
4. Have there been times when you needed to get yourself out of the way to see Christ present? Did things begin to change for you when you were able to see Christ more clearly?

Pray with me

Lord of life and light, help us to see you clearly with us. Let your love be visible in our lives; help us to reflect your glory. Open our eyes so we can see you near. Help us to remove any obstacle between us. Guide us to share your love with others and point the way to you. Brighten our hearts.

Ten

The Beloved Son

In those days Jesus came from Nazareth of Galilee and was baptized by John in the Jordan. And just as he was coming up out of the water, he saw the heavens torn apart and the Spirit descending like a dove on him. And a voice came from heaven, "You are my Son, the Beloved; with you I am well pleased." (Mark 1:9–11)

Jesus' public ministry begins with love. As he is baptized by John in the River Jordan, the divine voice from heaven proclaims Jesus to be the Son, the Beloved. The coming of Jesus into the world likewise begins with divine love: "For God so loved the world that he gave his only Son, so that everyone who believes in him may not perish but have eternal life" (John 3:16). The love of God is manifested dramatically at Jesus' baptism, and throughout his ministry.

Jesus is the Beloved. God the Father's love for the divine Son is unconditional. This is the perfect love that the divine Father and Son share with each other and offer to us, as Jesus prays for the disciples and those who believe in Him through them, "that they may all be one" (John 17:20–21). We are at one with God and we are beloved; God's love for us

190   Joy to the World!

is unconditional. There is no need for us to "qualify" for God's love. We have nothing to prove, no requirement to convince God to love us, and no need to wait for God's love to be awarded like a diploma for completed studies or a medal for good service. God's love comes first before anything we do. God's unconditional love is with us from the very beginning of our lives. Birth is a good time for unconditional love, as a parent first holds their child with overflowing affection, and the child is beloved.

We can also know and share God's love in our own choices. At each new beginning we can search our motivations. *Why* are we doing this; what *moves* us? Do we start a new conversation with love? Do we begin a new work with love? Do we reach out to another with love? Do we seek or begin a new direction with love? Do we commit our lives, give ourselves with love? We may find varied motives for whatever we choose and do, but at the heart of it all we should find *love*—God's love present and known in our loving responses, expressed in the moments and choices of our lives. We are beloved, and can help others to know and feel they are beloved.

Questions to ponder

1. Do your loved ones and friends know you believe in them? Do they know you are pleased by the good things in their lives?
2. Do your loved ones and friends feel your support and hope for them? Do you want the best for them?
3. Do you feel their belief in you and their support? Do they have hope for you?
4. Are they pleased by the good things in your life? Do they want the best for you?
5. When do you feel God is pleased with you? When do you feel God with you?

Pray with me

Blessed are you, Lord God, creator of our world and every living thing. Let us know and feel we are your beloved. Offer us your many gifts; let us share everything you give us. Surprise us with your love and invitations. Send us into your world with forgiveness, inspiration, and generosity. May we know your gifts better as we give them away. Let us help others know and feel they are your beloved. Help us to share your love.

Eleven

Come and see

Jesus decided to go to Galilee. He found Philip and said to him, "Follow me. Now Philip was from Bethsaida, the city of Andrew and Peter. Philip found Nathanael and said to him, "We have found him about whom Moses in the law and also the prophets wrote, Jesus son of Joseph from Nazareth." Nathanael said to him, "Can anything good come out of Nazareth?" Philip said to him, "Come and see." (John 1:43–46)

A glimpse of truth can sometimes cut through a lot of perspectives, theories, and even bias. The faith we share is a life to be lived, not a mere theory or an interesting idea to consider. Christ's life manifested in the world was an encounter with truth for many who saw and heard him. Nathanael may have doubted anything good could come out of Nazareth, but his viewpoint changed after meeting Jesus. Belief in Jesus replaced bias.

Sometimes appearances can be deceiving and assumptions can be wrong. Tragic consequences can follow. One summer I worked security for my university, and I was surprised to hear the security dispatcher report that a rabid dog was loose on a patient floor of the Vanderbilt hospital. So I went to see what was happening. When I arrived there was a group of medical staff and security on the inside of the door to a stairwell. Through a small window in the door I could see a medium-sized dog. He was sitting down and pleasantly looking up at the window. His mouth was frothy. He was hot. It was summer in Nashville and he was near an exit stair that was not well air-conditioned. On my side of the door a burly security policeman said, "That dog's rabid! I'm not going out there!" I said, "Stand back." I stepped through the door and the dog looked at me sweetly. He followed me down several flights of stairs and I let him out through the exit door. I gave a "mission complete" message to the dispatcher. It was fun. But I was glad to be the first person interacting with the harmless dog. Someone else might have hurt him. The people in a panic were totally convinced the dog was a serious threat. Their assumption was wrong, based on a misinterpretation of appearances. The dog was simply hot and thirsty.

It can be that way for us, too. Our bias, prejudice, and misinterpretation of appearances can blind us to moments of grace right before our eyes. Like Nathanael, we may be surprised to discover that amazing good can come from unexpected places and people.

Questions to ponder

1. When have you been surprised to discover God present and active in an unexpected place or person?
2. When have you seen God active in others or heard God's call through others?
3. When has bias or prejudice gotten in the way of faith for you? When has bias or prejudice prevented you from knowing another person?

Pray with me

Holy Lord, help us to let go of prejudice, bias, and any obstruction that separates us from you or others. Guide us to find you present and active in all kinds of people and places. Help us to see the truth about others and ourselves. Open our eyes and hearts. Help us to love generously as we receive graciously from you.

Twelve

The good wine

When the steward tasted the water that had become wine, and did not know where it came from (though the servants who had drawn the water knew), the steward called the bridegroom and said to him, "Everyone serves the good wine first, and then the inferior wine after the guests have become drunk. But you have kept the good wine until now." (John 2:9–10)

Jesus' first miracle saves the day at a wedding. The miracle at Cana did more than provide enough of the best wine for the wedding guests to drink. It also prevented the newlyweds from suffering a major humiliation. It would have been a failure of hospitality, a public shame, if there was not enough wine for the guests. Years later, people who knew them would remember the wedding banquet where the wine ran out, and some would probably still mention it, shaking their heads, wondering how it could have happened.

Some wounds and threats do not involve physical harm. Jesus' miracle saved a family's reputation, and prevented an embarrassing distraction at the celebration of the couple's wedding. It would not have been a good beginning for their marriage and life in that community. Their dilemma was not too small for Jesus' attention and help. He blessed their marriage and their family in an unexpected way. Jesus also blessed marriage itself. He "adorned this manner of life by his presence and first miracle at a wedding in Cana of Galilee," as noted in the celebrant's address to the congregation at the "Celebration and Blessing of a Marriage" (BCP, 423).

And, like many of Jesus' miracles, its significance went beyond an immediate need and its miraculous resolution to the essential truth of his life and mission. "Jesus did this, the first of his signs, in Cana of Galilee, and revealed his glory; and his disciples believed in him" (John 2:11). It was an epiphany that pointed his disciples and followers (and us) to belief in him whose miracles were gifts of love. It was a reminder that God is present with us always; every day we can see moments of epiphany. It also reminds us to take another's concern seriously, whether or not we share their concern.

Questions to ponder

1. *What has pointed you in the direction of faith? Has this happened in unexpected situations or ways?*
2. *How have you known God present in your life? Have you found unexpected help in a time of need or embarrassment?*
3. *Have you found God present with you in a joyful time of celebration?*
4. *Have you found God present in your daily routine and everyday concerns? How?*

Pray with me

Blessed are you, Lord Jesus Christ, you reveal your glory in the world and love generously. Draw near when we need you. Be with us every day in all the moments of our lives. Help us to know you are present when we are lost or confused. Remind us of your love when we are anxious or embarrassed. Give us peace. Share our times of joy; celebrate with us. Be the light in our hearts.

Thirteen

Follow me

As he walked by the Sea of Galilee, he saw two brothers, Simon, who is called Peter, and Andrew his brother, casting a net into the sea—for they were fishermen. And he said to them, "Follow me, and I will make you fish for people." Immediately they left their nets and followed him." As he went from there, he saw two other brothers, James son of Zebedee and his brother John, in the boat with their father Zebedee, mending their nets, and he called them. Immediately they left the boat and their father, and followed him. (Mark 1:16–20)

An *immediate* response can be unequivocal, without distraction or hesitation, a total and heartfelt expression of faith. St. Benedict notes in his *Rule* (5.1–10) that faithful obedience should be without delay. We see an immediate response by Simon and Andrew, James and John when Jesus invites them to leave their work as fishermen to follow him and "fish for people." Immediately they leave their nets and everything familiar to them. No weighing of benefits and risks, positives and negatives. They step out of their boats and the life they know to follow Jesus. They trust him.

We see other immediate responses in the New Testament. When Jesus heals Simon's mother-in-law, she immediately gets up and serves (Luke

4:38–39). Jesus also heals a woman who was bent over and had been disabled for eighteen years. Immediately she stands up straight and praises God (Luke 13:11–13). Saul on the way to Damascus is confronted by the risen Lord and blinded by a heavenly light. He is healed by Ananias. After several days with the disciples in Damascus, Saul immediately begins to proclaim Jesus in the synagogues (Acts 9:1–20).

We also can respond *immediately* to Jesus' invitation, no matter how we receive or discern his call to follow. We can let go of weighing every pro and con; we can act *now* in faith and follow our Lord. Like the fishermen who became disciples, we can embrace faith and an unknown future without delay or hesitation. Instead of holding back we can give ourselves with love. Moments of epiphany can prompt our immediate response in faith and love.

Questions to ponder

1. When have you accepted God's invitation to respond? When have you responded "immediately"? What was different about that situation relative to other times?
2. Have there been times when you wished your response was immediate? Why did you hesitate?
3. Have there been times when it would have been important to wait, or you needed time to decide?
4. When have you chosen to give up something to accept an important invitation or opportunity? When has this meant a real sacrifice for you?

Pray with me

Dear Lord, our life-giver, call us and we will follow immediately. Show us the way and we will go with you. Never leave us. Guide us and we will understand. Open our eyes and we will see. Speak and we will hear your voice. Knock, and we will open to you. Give and we will share.

Fourteen

A new teaching

[Jesus and his disciples] went to Capernaum; and when the sabbath came, he entered the synagogue and taught. They were astounded at this teaching, for he taught them as one having authority, and not as the scribes. Just then there was in their synagogue a man with an unclean spirit, and he cried out, "What have you to do with us, Jesus of Nazareth? Have you come to destroy us? I know who you are, the Holy One of God." But Jesus rebuked him, saying, "Be silent, and come out of him!" And the unclean spirit, convulsing him and crying with a loud voice, came out of him. They were all amazed, and they kept on asking one another, "What is this? A new teaching—with authority! He commands even the unclean spirits, and they obey him." (Mark 1:21–27)

Jesus astounds the people with what he says and does. He teaches and acts with *authority*. His power amazes them. Even the unclean spirit recognizes him. Jesus' authority is manifest.

The word "authority" has several meanings. Authority can mean the power to give orders. An Army general has authority to order soldiers into battle; the police have authority to arrest a criminal suspect. But Jesus expresses his authority differently. He never takes away our free will or ability

202   Joy to the World!

to choose. Jesus certainly has the power of authority, but he consistently seeks to invite, attract, explain, persuade, and include. "Force is not of God" (F. Bland Tucker, "The great creator of the worlds," v. 5, Hymn 489, from *Epistle to Diognetus,* circa 150, trans. F. Bland Tucker).

At the time of his arrest Jesus urges one of his followers to put away his sword instead of defending him with violence. Jesus warns that "all who take the sword will perish by the sword," and he asks, "Do you think that I cannot appeal to my Father, and he will at once send me more than twelve legions of angels?" (Matt. 26:52–53) Jesus has that authority, but he does not use it to protect himself.

To be an authority suggests authentic expertise. Jesus *is* the ultimate authority concerning the life of faith and salvation in God. He knows what he is talking about and what he is doing. We can trust his words, accept his guidance, follow his example. Authority is also creative, power to *author,* to create a new thing, to reshape and renew. Jesus authors a new way to live, a new path of hope, a new outcome for those who walk in his love. His creative power is manifest in what he does and says—astounding people, casting out an evil spirit, authoring our salvation.

Questions to ponder

1. How do you know God's authority in your life? How does faith shape the meaning of authority for you?
2. Have there been moments when you came to see things differently because of faith?
3. Have you been surprised to realize you could go beyond limitations that seemed permanent?
4. When have you found new or unexpected hope? Have you discovered a new beginning?

Pray with me

God of mercy, help us know you present in each day. Create in us a new heart. Show us what is possible with faith in you. Surprise us with grace. Help us discover new possibilities and move into them. Always draw us closer to you. Open the doors of your love.

Fifteen

Be made clean

A leper came to [Jesus] begging him, and kneeling he said to him, "If you choose, you can make me clean." Moved with pity, Jesus stretched out his hand and touched him, and said to him, "I do choose. Be made clean." Immediately the leprosy left him, and he was made clean. (Mark 1:40–42)

People with leprosy were outcasts in Jesus' day—isolated, excluded, untouchable, rejected as sinners. But Jesus did not avoid the person with leprosy who knelt before him and begged for his help. Jesus did not reject him because of his illness.

I had chicken pox as an adult. I never had it as a child but caught it from my daughter Claire when she was about two years old and came home with chicken pox from daycare. She had a mild case with only a few sores and a low-grade fever. I felt like I had sores over every inch of my body. I was miserable, feverish, and quarantined. But I was working on a project, and my collaborator needed my materials. He previously had chicken pox and was not worried about being exposed to it. So he came to my apartment to pick up the papers. He did not say anything when he saw my face, but it was as if he took a full step back when he saw me.

For just a moment his expression suggested a whiff of disgust that hurt in the pit of my stomach. I felt unclean, untouchable, separated from the world of healthy people whose faces were not marked with sores. It was a bad feeling.

Jesus was not disgusted by the man with leprosy or afraid to touch him. Jesus did not dismiss the sick man as a sinner. Jesus was moved with compassion for him. It was Jesus' will and choice to heal him instead of turning away. Jesus chose to stretch out his hand and touch what society had deemed an untouchable person. Jesus touched his heart.

Jesus crossed the boundaries and disregarded the expectations of his society to minister when needed. With a touch to heal, Jesus reached beyond common prejudices and judgments based on appearance. He healed the man with leprosy and brought him into the world of the living. The man would no longer be confined to the margins of the world he knew; he was no longer untouchable. Jesus opened a place for him in society with others and freedom to explore. Jesus welcomed him with love.

Questions to ponder

*1. Are there "untouchables" in your world—
people you avoid or refuse to help?
2. Have you stepped outside conventional
expectations to help someone else?
3. Have you helped others when they needed
healing? Were you helped by helping them?
4. Have you known Christ's presence while
experiencing your own healing?*

Pray with me

Holy One, Lord of life, touch us for healing. Strengthen us for service; let us help everyone you love. Guide us to reach past prejudices and appearances to comfort others who are isolated or in pain. Draw us to the fullness of life in you. May your light be visible in us.

Sixteen

Not condemned

Have you not known? Have you not heard? The Lord is the everlasting God, the Creator of the ends of the earth. He does not faint or grow weary; his understanding is unsearchable. He gives power to the faint, and strengthens the powerless. Even youths will faint and be weary, and the young will fall exhausted; but those who wait for the Lord shall renew their strength, they shall mount up with wings like eagles, they shall run and not be weary, they shall walk and not faint. (Isa. 40:28–31)

It was a hot and humid Fourth of July in Atlanta, Georgia, and I was running the 10K Peachtree Road Race with my wife Victoria. It was a huge event with tens of thousands of runners and walkers, and spectators lining the downtown streets of the city. Unfortunately in the crowd of spectators for this race (and others I have run), I could see a "religious" sign filled with condemnations and threats of severe judgment in a too-hot place that was waiting for me if I did not change my ways. I was already well aware of my physical limitations as I did my best to toil up the hills of that race course on a day that was already plenty hot in Atlanta. The last thing I needed was the added weight of a condemnation, much less one delivered in the name of the Almighty.

But there was a moment of relief and hope for me in the Peachtree Road Race, and I was never prouder to be an Episcopalian. The race course goes by the Episcopal Cathedral of St. Philip after the second mile of the race. And there it was, on the right side of the race course and in sight of the Cathedral—an Episcopal water station! Clergy and perhaps others from the Cathedral were passing out cups of water. I also remember a cooling station with a shower of water for runners to pass through, and one clergyman sprinkling (asperging) the runners with holy water as they ran by. It was beautiful, and fun. Literally, it was cool. Instead of being condemned and threatened, I felt blessed.

Christ does not come into our world to condemn us. Our Lord does not seek to win us over by intimidation or causing fear. He comes with love, not threats. He comes to raise us up, not to put us down. He comes to share His life with us and make us equals with him. In Christ we have salvation; we are His friends, His family, His body. Christ renews our strength and gives us hope.

At the limits of our own strength and control we may clearly discover our need for God. We are made for help beyond ourselves. We cannot save ourselves; we cannot complete ourselves. We need everything our Lord gives us. God lifts us beyond ourselves with call, inspiration, forgiveness, gifts, and power to serve. Our Lord guides us; we can see a new way forward in Him. God knows each of us, understands our needs, and stands with us. Grace revives and refreshes us, bringing us to life. We discover strength within us that is beyond our own; we discover God with us. In Christ we may run and not be weary, we may walk and not faint.

Questions to ponder

1. How has God renewed your body and spirit?
2. When have you found hope in a situation that seemed hopeless?
3. When have you discovered strength in a time of vulnerability and confusion?
4. Has a path opened for you when there seemed to be no way forward?

Pray with Me

Hear us, Lord; come quickly to help. Come with mercy to forgive us. Come with healing to restore us. Come with strength to empower us. Come with inspiration to excite our minds and move our hearts. Come with guidance to call us to action and give us purpose. Raise us up. Let us serve others and share your love. May every step draw us nearer to you and those you love. Let us run and not be weary; let us walk and not faint.

Seventeen

New wine

"No one sews a piece of unshrunk cloth on an old cloak; otherwise, the patch pulls away from it, the new from the old, and a worse tear is made. And no one puts new wine into old wineskins; otherwise, the wine will burst the skins, and the wine is lost, and so are the skins; but one puts new wine into fresh wineskins." (Mark 2:21–22)

Sometimes we get stuck in old ruts, clinging to old excuses, and holding onto the past like old wine in worn-out wineskins. But Jesus invites us into an adventure of faith, a life renewed through fresh ways of serving, understanding, and healing. Our Lord calls us to step onto new roads, to open our eyes, and to embrace the transformation He offers. In Christ, we are made new (Rev. 21:5).

A friend once told me about how trappers in South America capture monkeys for zoos without harming them. They hollow out a gourd, carving a hole just big enough for a monkey to slip its paw inside. They place enticing nuts inside the gourd and secure it to the ground. The monkey looking for food will slip a paw into the gourd and grab the nuts. But the monkey's clinched paw is too big to slip out of the gourd while holding the nuts. The monkey can leave at any time by dropping the nuts and scurrying away. But the monkey wants the nuts and will not leave; the monkey is trapped!

Like the monkey, we can trap ourselves by clinging to habits, perspectives, or ways of living that no longer serve us. We can hold tightly to what is familiar, even when it blocks us from the fullness of life in Christ. We may find ourselves protecting and holding on to our biggest obstacles, the very things that hurt us and hold us back. But freedom is within our grasp—all we need to do is let go. When we release what holds us back, we create space for God to renew us, lead us forward, and fill us with His new life.

Questions to ponder

1. *Are you stuck in an old rut? Do you need to let go of something?*
2. *Are you ready for something new? Are you open to a fresh perspective, a new way of being or doing, a discovery?*
3. *How can you make a fresh start? What will be your new beginning?*
4. *What are your first steps to make a difference?*

Pray with me

Blessed are you, Lord God, creator of all that is and each of us; you make all things new. Lift us out of discouragement and fatigue. Renew our hearts and minds. Help us to let go of whatever separates us from you. Open our eyes to see your love surrounding us. Let us give generously as we receive from you. Quicken our hearts and hands to share your love. Let us find new life in you.

Eighteen

God with us through every danger

But now thus says the Lord, he who created you, O Jacob, he who formed you, O Israel: Do not fear, for I have redeemed you; I have called you by name, you are mine. When you pass through the waters, I will be with you; and through the rivers, they shall not overwhelm you; when you walk through fire you shall not be burned, and the flame shall not consume you. For I am the Lord your God, the Holy One of Israel, your Savior. (Isa. 43:1–7)

"Fear not" is one of the most frequently repeated assurances in the Bible. Fear not, Mary, when the archangel announces to you; fear not, shepherds, when you hear the herald of Good News; fear not, followers of Jesus, when anxious about persecution or the authorities, or having enough; fear not, believers, when facing the risen Lord himself; fear not when facing situations in life that are unexpected, confusing, disappointing, threatening, or hurtful.

Fear not, even in the valley of the shadow of death, because God is with us and surrounds us with love (Psalm 23:4). St. Paul states that nothing

God with us through every danger 213

will separate us from the love of Christ and we are "more than conquerors" in all hardships and perils because "neither death, nor life, nor angels, nor rulers, nor things present, nor things to come, nor powers, nor height, nor depth, nor anything else in all creation, will be able to separate us from the love of God in Christ Jesus our Lord" (Romans 8:35–39).

Jonathan Daniels, an Episcopal seminarian martyred during the civil rights movement in 1965, stated he "lost fear" in Alabama "when I began to know in my bones and sinews that I had truly been baptized into the Lord's death and Resurrection, that in the only sense that really matters I am already dead, and my life is hid with Christ in God" (Jonathan Daniels, "June 22, 1965," in William J. Schneider, *American Martyr: The Jon Daniels Story*).

Our life in God, the love we share, the peace we know when there is no peace in the world around us, the strength of Christ's life upholding us, divine hands that will not let us go—this is the basis of our trust in the face of death and every threat. This is our blessed assurance. Nothing will come between us and the love of God that overcomes the fears of our heart. "In returning and rest you shall be saved; in quietness and in trust shall be your strength" (Isa. 30:15). We can trust that God is with us and for us in every fearful moment. We can let go of whatever undermines our assurance; we can *live.*

Questions to ponder

1. Have you felt God's presence in your life? Do you trust that God is with you?
2. Have you discovered God present in times of trial or difficulty, or at other times?
3. Have you been present for others in their times of need, or received needed help from others?

Pray with me

Lord of peace, quiet my heart, calm my fears, draw me near. Walk with me always. Guide me through dangers and storms. Share my celebrations and every day. Let me find my place with you.

Nineteen

Knowing Christ

"Come, you that are blessed by my Father, inherit the kingdom prepared for you from the foundation of the world; for I was hungry and you gave me food, I was thirsty and you gave me something to drink, I was a stranger and you welcomed me, I was naked and you gave me clothing, I was in prison and you visited me. . . . Truly I tell you, just as you did it to one of the least of these who are members of my family, you did it to me." (Matt. 25:34–36, 40)

On my first day of theology class in seminary, Fr. James Griffiss wrote a five-word question in chalk on the blackboard: "How do we know God?" His question has many answers, and I continue to work on it.

We can know God through other people. We can know God constantly through the circumstances of life we encounter in each day. This is an incarnational spirituality. We believe God is active in our world. Every moment offers an opportunity to discover God with us, the extraordinary presence of God in the ordinary situations of our daily lives. There is a sacramentality to this, although not always involving an official Sacrament of the Church. God can be known in creation, in things and creatures we encounter regularly in life—people, situations, the beauty and order of nature, as well as water, bread, wine, oil.

216   Joy to the World!

The first word of *The Rule of St. Benedict* is "Listen" (Prologue 1). We can more readily discern God's presence if our hearts and senses are open, allowing us to listen (literally and figuratively) for God with us in each moment. Listening acknowledges we do not have all the answers in ourselves; we need to receive from beyond ourselves. Benedict's *Rule* was written "to establish a school for the Lord's service" (*The Rule of St. Benedict*, Prologue 45), knowing Christ through a shared community life that balanced prayer, work, and study. Everything happening in community life is for the sake of knowing God, not just for the sake of an efficient or productive community.

Benedict's *Rule* provides guidance for many ways of knowing God in any community, including direction for welcoming guests with hospitality and an open heart: "All guests who arrive should be received as Christ, for he himself will say, *I was a stranger and you took me in*" (*Rule of St. Benedict* 53.1; Matt. 25:35). In Benedict's time, all kinds of people—pilgrims, travelers, wanderers—would arrive at the monastery without reservations, seeking welcome, a place to stay, perhaps seeking God. In this time of "poor communications and lack of hotels and inns, monasteries were often the only place where one could find a safe place to stay for the night" (Kardong, *Benedict's Rule, A Translation and Commentary*). Benedict's direction is to welcome *all* (Latin, *omnes*), to include all in the hospitality of the community. This is radical hospitality.

Guests may arrive at "odd hours" (*Rule of St. Benedict*, 53.16). Benedict takes steps to make sure the arriving guests will be welcomed, and to avoid disruption of community life. He designates a porter to be stationed at the monastery gate with quarters near the gate to welcome those who arrive at any time (*Rule of St. Benedict*, 66.1–2). The visitor is not an intrusion on the orderly life of the community; the visitor comes as a gift, an opportunity to know Christ by offering hospitality to that person, and to find Christ in that person. Christ is encountered when the guest is welcomed; Christ is served when the guest is fed. Christ "is in fact the one who is received"

(*Rule of St. Benedict*, 53.7). This is a moment of epiphany. We also can know God through the people we meet and serve in the many contexts of our lives. We can know Christ as we share His love with others.

Questions to ponder

1. When and how have you come to know Christ?
2. Have you known Christ through other people?
3. Have you found Christ present in everyday situations of life? When?
4. Have you found Christ present in a relationship, a family, a church, a community, an organization? When?
5. Have you found Christ present in acts of service, helping others, welcoming others to your church or community?
6. Has radical hospitality led to unexpected opportunities and challenges for you, your church, your community?

Pray with me

Loving God, be known to us in the people we meet and serve. Help us to be generous with the love you share. Let us find you present in every moment of our lives. Open our hearts; help us to listen for you. May we know your love as we share your love; may we know your healing as we help others to heal. Kindle our hearts as we share encouragement and hope in your name. May all our service draw us closer to you and everyone we serve.

Twenty

Good News

[Jesus] came to his hometown and began to teach the people in their synagogue, so that they were astounded and said, "Where did this man get this wisdom and these deeds of power? Is not this the carpenter's son? Is not his mother called Mary? And are not his brothers James and Joseph and Simon and Judas? And are not all his sisters with us? Where then did this man get all this?" And they took offense at him. But Jesus said to them, "Prophets are not without honor except in their own country and in their own house." And he did not do many deeds of power there, because of their unbelief. (Matt. 13:54–58)

Jesus comes to the synagogue in his hometown on the sabbath and he reads Isaiah's prophecy concerning the expected coming of the Messiah. The Christ, the Anointed One, will proclaim Good News to the poor, release for the captives, recovery of sight for the blind, freedom for the oppressed; the Messiah will proclaim the year of the Lord's favor (Luke 4:16–19). This was usual behavior for a Jewish rabbi, and Jesus was fulfilling the expectations of a rabbi. He was in the synagogue on the sabbath; he was in the right place at the right time. And he proceeded to teach the congregation based on the scripture text that he read to them. Again, very

Good News

usual behavior for a rabbi; a scene that was similar to others happening in many synagogues on that day.

But then things took a very unexpected turn. Jesus applied Isaiah's messianic prophecy to *himself*: "Today this scripture has been fulfilled in your hearing" (Luke 4:21)! This claim was *not* happening in other synagogues on that day! Jesus went beyond his role of rabbi to claim his own vocation as the Messiah, the Anointed One, the Christ. It was an epiphany, a clear and most unexpected self-revelation by Jesus.

This would have been a shocking moment in any synagogue, but especially in Jesus's hometown. His visit to the synagogue in Nazareth may have been one of the biggest challenges in his early ministry. The people there thought they knew him and seriously doubted that this man—this boy they had watched grow up—had a higher calling. They asked incredulously, "Is this not Joseph's son?" (Luke 4:22) They rejected him.

The people in the Nazareth synagogue thought they knew where Jesus fit into the scheme of things in their town. They became indignant when he announced his true identity and mission; they saw him very differently, based on what they knew of him. The release, recovery, freedom, and fulfillment of the Messiah's coming was presented right before their eyes and in their hearing. But they refused to accept it. Jesus knew his truth and was undeterred by their misunderstanding of him. He knew who he was, even if he was not honored in his own hometown. His mission continued.

Questions to ponder

1. Have prejudice and bias prevented you from appreciating another's gifts or collaborating with them? Have prejudice and bias prevented others from appreciating your gifts or collaborating with you?
2. Have you misunderstood another or dismissed their gifts? Have others misunderstood you at times or dismissed your gifts? Have you encountered obstacles or barriers to your ministry?
3. Have you helped another find release from something that was hurting them? Has another helped you to find release from something that was hurting you?
4. Have you known freedom, recovery, healing in Christ?

Pray with me

Holy One, source of healing, free us and release us from every harm. May we remove every obstacle between us and you. Help us to see others for who they are, and help others to see us for who we are. May we all work together. Guide us to move forward and use our gifts. Fulfill our love. Help us proclaim the Good News of life in you. Let us share freedom, recovery, and healing.

Twenty-One

Let down your nets

When [Jesus] had finished speaking, he said to Simon, "Put out into the deep water and let down your nets for a catch." Simon answered, "Master, we have worked all night long but have caught nothing. Yet if you say so, I will let down the nets." When they had done this, they caught so many fish that their nets were beginning to break. (Luke 5:4–6)

Jesus invites Simon to believe in Him, to take his suggestion for better fishing, and to persist despite his earlier lack of success. I expect Simon looked at Jesus with total disbelief when Jesus told him to put out into the deep and keep fishing. Simon and the other fishermen worked all night on the lake of Gennesaret and they caught nothing. They did their best, they worked very hard, but their efforts yielded nothing. Another try seemed hopeless. But, fortunately for him, Simon was willing to listen and he acted on Jesus' direction. Peter and the other fishermen caught so many fish their boats were sinking (Luke 5:7). They persisted.

The Christian life calls for persistence. Dorothy Day once wrote, "The longer I am in the apostolate the more I am sure perseverance and constancy are the two great needs." Humorously, she also once wrote

222 Joy to the World!

Thomas Merton that "My constant prayer is for final perseverance—to go on as I am trusting always the Lord Himself will take me by the hair of the head like Habakkuk and set me where he wants me" (Dorothy Day, *All the Way to Heaven*)(See Bel and the Dragon, 1:33–36). Dorothy did her best to persist in following our Lord despite obstacles and failures.

Sometimes we may fail, but we are still called to respond in faith. We can be relentless for the Gospel, we can persist. Proverbs (24:16) says of the righteous, "though they fall seven times, they will rise again." I once fell hard in a half marathon in Omaha and was not sure I could get up. First I stood, then I walked, then I ran again. The Jewish text *Pirkei Avot* (*Ethics of the Fathers,* 2:16) states that "you are not obligated to complete the task, but neither are you free to abandon it."

Simon and the other fishermen discovered the depths of power, truth, and love in Jesus' words. At his direction they tried again instead of giving up. It was an epiphany for them and us. Their nets were breaking with an astounding catch of fish, and their lives were changing as Jesus showed a new path forward. It was costly grace for them. They left everything to follow Jesus and share his life of faith. They would fish for people, and they would live to catch and save many. Despite opposition and many obstacles, they would persist.

Questions to ponder

1. When have you persisted to do something important despite lack of initial success, opposition, or obstacles? Were you tempted to give up when you were unsuccessful at first?
2. What helped you to try again when you needed persistence to complete an important goal? How did the help you received make a difference for you?
3. Has someone helped you to stand when you fell? What help did you receive? Have you helped another to stand when they fell? What help did you give?
4. Has faith helped you to persist when you needed to complete an important commitment or goal? What gave you hope?

Pray with me

Blessed are you, Lord God, our savior, healer, and guide. Help us to stand when we fall. Show us the path forward when we are confused and discouraged. Draw near to help us. Renew our faith and hope as we strive to follow wherever you lead us. Surprise us with unexpected adventures of faith. Let us hear your call. Help us to receive the gifts you offer. Strengthen us to overcome fear that holds us back, even fear of failure. Let us find our way in you. Help us to persist in your love.

Twenty-Two

A variety of gifts

Now there are varieties of gifts, but the same Spirit; and there are varieties of services, but the same Lord; and there are varieties of activities, but it is the same God who activates all of them in everyone. To each is given the manifestation of the Spirit for the common good. (1 Cor. 12:4–7)

At my kindergarten "graduation," all the kids were supposed to find a seat on stage while their parents and relatives were looking on proudly. Underneath our chairs was a musical instrument; we would sing a song at the end of the ceremony. Going in, we were unsure exactly where we would sit or which instrument we would find. The instruments had to be something we could pick up and play—tambourines, bells, drums, horns. The instrument under each chair was a surprise, like an unexpected gift. We ended up making many different sounds, but somehow it blended together.

It is also possible to discover our spiritual gifts with surprise. At some point, we may realize there is something we do well, and there is a need for us to do it. We may have to work hard at it, receive instruction, but there is also something about our gift that was not taught or learned. The gift was there from the beginning, as if waiting to be discovered, polished, and used.

A variety of gifts

We may also realize our gift is as much for others as for us—maybe more for others than us. The gift is meant to be shared, not hidden or reserved for convenient times. Sometimes our gifts may be needed in situations or times we did not choose.

There are varieties of gifts and services but they come from the same Lord (1 Cor. 12:4-5). God's love, God's presence moving in our lives can be manifested through our gifts. We each have many gifts. And it is wonderful to be with people who have different gifts. The body of Christ has many members (1 Cor. 12:12). The myriad gifts we share are complementary. At times we may receive others' help in areas that are not our gifts; we may do the same for them. Every tax season I am very grateful for my accountant's skill!

Our gifts can provide small moments of epiphany that draw us together in shared service and offered help, pointing us beyond ourselves and the demands of a particular situation to the Giver of all our gifts. We know our gifts best when we use them—serving, discerning, teaching, reconciling, exploring, administering, caring, leading, creating, listening, supporting, healing, preaching, providing, and more! Our gifts can be the most direct path to our hearts, near to our deepest sense of who we are. Our gifts can also be our point of closest connection with others, drawing us together

Questions to ponder

1. What are your gifts? How have you used them?
2. Have you been surprised to discover unexpected gifts?
3. Have you been helped by others' gifts?
4. Have you helped others to discern and share their gifts?
5. Do you have gifts you hope to use more fully in the future? How?

with them and the source of all our gifts, manifesting God's presence with us for life and the common good.

Pray with me

Generous Lord, giver of all our gifts, lover of souls, we thank you for your many gifts to us. Open our eyes to see you active and moving in our lives through your gifts. Help us to discern our gifts and use them graciously. Let us help others to discover and share their gifts. Draw us nearer to you as we offer our gifts in love.

Twenty-Three

Love your enemies

Love your enemies, do good to those who hate you, bless those who curse you, pray for those who abuse you. If anyone strikes you on the cheek, offer the other also; and from anyone who takes away your coat do not withhold even your shirt. Give to everyone who begs from you; and if anyone takes away your goods, do not ask for them again. Do to others as you would have them do to you. (Luke 6:27–31)

Jesus' divinity was clearly meant to be seen by the disciples who were with him on the mountaintop at the Transfiguration. And Jesus' divinity was manifest at other times in his ministry—his healings and other miracles, his preaching and teaching, and his sacrifice. It may not be difficult to recognize God's presence in the lives of the saints, and of those we love. But we may be surprised to discover God present in the lives of those we struggle with, those we find difficult, even our adversaries or enemies. God who loves us also loves them, and so can we. Indeed, Jesus directs us to love our enemies. Can we obey? Will we? Dorothy Day often said "we love God as much as the one we love the least" (Dorothy Day, *All the Way to Heaven*).

228   Joy to the World!

We can find an example of love for the enemy in the extreme circumstances of war. Geoffrey Studdert-Kennedy ("Woodbine Willie"), an Anglican priest, British Army chaplain in World War I, and writer of theological reflections, recalls the big guns firing on the enemy on the morning of the attack on the Messines–Wytschaete Ridge, June 7, 1917. He says the guns were loud and at first the other soldiers were laughing: "That's the stuff to give 'em. It is a glorious sight, one silver sheet of leaping flame against the blackness of the trees." Then Studdert-Kennedy sees the situation differently: "But it's damnable, it's a disgrace to civilization. It's murder. . . . They have wives and kiddies like my Patrick, and they are being torn to bits and tortured" (Studdert-Kennedy, "What is God like?" in *The Hardest Part*). Studdert-Kennedy's focus moves with empathy and compassion from the sights and sounds of a big attack to a horrified realization of the human consequences—death and suffering—being faced by the enemy at that time. He remembers the enemy soldiers have families of their own, including children like his own son. He shares the pain of the enemy soldiers. He realizes what he has in common with the enemy instead of seeing only their threat and the harm they have done.

We also may discover more in common with our enemies than we expected. A fresh and unbiased perspective on people who annoy or oppose us may let us find common ground, reconcile, and get along. It can help if we understand the history of a situation, including the other's needs and what motivates them. How we treat our enemies can be a telling measure of authentic Christian faith.

Questions to ponder

1. How do you treat people who are difficult to be around or hard to like?
2. Do you try to find common ground with them or work through differences that obstruct a relationship?
3. Have you ever reconciled with an enemy?
4. What made a difference to improve the situation? Were the first steps toward reconciliation awkward?
5. How does faith shape the way you treat others when there is disagreement or alienation?

Pray with me

Holy One, Lord of peace, guide us to treat others with care and respect. Help us to love those who do not love us. Help us to find you in the most difficult people and situations. Let us seek and draw out the best in others. Guide us to resolve quarrels instead of aggravating conflicts. Help us to take the first steps toward reconciliation, and to continue. Let us heal divisions, broken relationships, and splintered communities whenever possible. Give us peace.

Twenty-Four

The Word of God fulfilled

Seek the Lord while he wills to be found; call upon him when he draws near. Let the wicked forsake their ways and the evil ones their thoughts; And let them turn to the Lord, and he will have compassion, and to our God, for he will richly pardon. . . . For as rain and snow fall from the heavens and return not again, but water the earth, Bringing forth life and giving growth, seed for sowing and bread for eating, So is my word that goes forth from my mouth; it will not return to me empty; But it will accomplish that which I have purposed, and prosper in that for which I sent it. (Isa. 55:6–7, 10–11; BCP, Canticle 10, 87–87)

We may know God is always near, but we may experience God's presence most powerfully in times of need when our limitations are obvious, and at times when God's presence is manifested in our lives. We may discern God's presence in synchronous moments when one door opens as another closes. We may know God with us when we are surprised by grace, answered prayers, or a solution for problems that seemed impossible to resolve.

Our outward experience may itself be like a sacrament, even if it is not an official Sacrament of the Church. We may see an outward and visible

The Word of God fulfilled

sign of the inward, spiritual, dynamic, moving presence of God in our lives. We may see epiphanies of God's presence in every day. The abundance, power, and plenty of God can be seen in the rain and snow that water the earth, providing "seed for sowing and bread for eating," nourishing the fullness of life.

Natural beauty reminds us of God's presence and moves our hearts to praise. In the hymn "Earth and all stars," Herbert F. Brokering exults, "Hail, wind, and rain, loud blowing snowstorms, sing to the Lord a new song! Flowers and trees, loud rustling dry leaves, sing to the Lord a new song!" Brokering's refrain for this hymn is filled with praise for God: "He has done marvelous things. I, too, will praise him with a new song!" (Hymn 412, v. 2 and refrain) Natural beauty points us to the Source of all beauty, filling us with awe and wonder. An evening hymn gives praise and worship to God through images of nature in day and night: "Christ, mighty Savior, Light of all creation, you make the daytime radiant with the sunlight and to the night give glittering adornment, stars in the heavens" ("Christ, mighty Savior," Hymn 33, v. 1, from the Mozarabic, tenth century, trans. Alan G. McDougall). Nature in all its beauty can draw our hearts and minds to heaven, assuring us that God is near.

Despite challenges and obstacles, we can find God active in our world, our neighbors, and ourselves. We can forgive and be forgiven. We can share the generosity and love we have received. We can know the glory of the Lord who is reflected in the beauty and majesty of nature that surrounds us, a spectacular epiphany. We can discover God with us and give thanks.

Questions to ponder

1. When have you found God present in your life? Have you seen God active in the life of someone else?
2. Is God's love visible in your life? Have you been an epiphany for someone else?
3. Have you been reminded of God's presence by the beauty and order of nature? When?
4. How has God's presence in your life changed you?

Pray with me

Draw near, O Lord, and hear our cry. Heal our wounds, give us strength. Guide us forward to know, love, and serve. Come down like rain and snow from the heavens; be present with us. Fill our hearts with your love, deliver us from sin and hurt, let us find completion and fulfillment in you. Help us to share your abundance. Raise our eyes to your glory.

Twenty-Five

Transfigured

Jesus took with him Peter and James and John, and led them up a high mountain apart, by themselves. And he was transfigured before them, and his clothes became dazzling white, such as no one on earth could bleach them. And there appeared to them Elijah with Moses, who were talking with Jesus. . . . Then a cloud overshadowed them, and from the cloud there came a voice, 'This is my Son, the Beloved; listen to him!' Suddenly when they looked around, they saw no one with them any more, but only Jesus. (Mark 9:2–4, 7–8)

Peter, James, and John were with Jesus on the holy mountain at the Transfiguration, and they were overwhelmed by everything they saw and heard. They see Jesus transfigured before them in glory, his clothes dazzling white. Icons of the Transfiguration often show them to be literally bowled over, off balance, on the ground in the presence of their transfigured Lord. The glorified Christ is revealed, and his closest disciples seem small and confused in comparison.

Peter would have erected booths for Jesus, Moses, and Elijah; Peter's misunderstanding of this great scene is obvious. From the overshadowing cloud on the mountain the voice of God declares that Jesus is his *Beloved*

234   Joy to the World!

Son. He fulfills and surpasses both the law of Moses and the prophetic tradition represented by Elijah. This divine declaration of the Beloved Son's identity is heard at the beginning and near the end of Jesus' earthly ministry. He will soon face the cross. The Transfiguration can also be a reminder of hope for the disciples and others who will encounter dark days in the near future. They will not forget Christ in glory. Neither should we.

The Transfiguration prefigures the resurrected glory of the risen Christ. We have no biblical account of the Resurrection itself, but we see Jesus in glory on the holy mountain. This is the ultimate epiphany in His ministry. Christ in glory also prefigures the resurrected glory that we may share in Him. His glory is our hope. On the Last Sunday after the Epiphany (a day when we hear the Transfiguration story), we pray "that we, beholding by faith the light of Christ's countenance, may be strengthened to bear our cross, and be changed into His likeness from glory to glory" (BCP, 217).

We bow before Christ's transcendent mystery revealed for us. The Transfiguration adds nothing to Jesus' divinity. He is fully God and fully human from the beginning of his incarnate life. But the Transfiguration adds much to our knowing the Christ in glory and our hope for life in Him. The Transfiguration is a spectacular epiphany of the glorified Christ, a thundering declaration by the Father of Christ's divine identity, and an invitation for us to follow Christ, "the pioneer and perfecter of our faith" (Heb. 12:2), who opens for us the way to sharing the life and love of God.

Behold the glory of the Lord. The light of Christ fills the sky. The God of glory thunders. This is the Son; *listen.* The glory of God shakes the trees in the forest. The light of Christ opens eyes and hearts. Christ's glory is dazzling, brilliant. On the mountaintop he is transfigured. In the light of Christ we see truth and hope revealed; we find new life. Holy God, share your blazing love; *transfigure us!*

Questions to ponder

1. Has Christ dazzled you? Has Christ surpassed your expectations?
2. Have you been transformed? What is your hope? Do you see a new horizon of possibility for yourself in Christ?
3. Has your life taken a new direction? What has made a difference for you?
4. What has changed for you because of faith in Christ? Have you known His glory?
5. Have you been amazed to discover new perspectives and hope? Do others see a change in you?

Pray with me

O Christ, Lord and God, show your dazzling brightness and reveal your glory in the world. Surround us with your brilliant love. Bring your light and life to heal us. Open our hearts; renew our hope. May your radiant light be visible in us; let us share your love.

Twenty-Six

Get up!

Suddenly there appeared to them Moses and Elijah, talking with him. Then Peter said to Jesus, "Lord, it is good for us to be here; if you wish I will make three dwellings here, one for you, one for Moses, and one for Elijah." While he was still speaking, suddenly a bright cloud overshadowed them, and from the cloud a voice said, "This is my Son, the Beloved; with him I am well pleased; listen to him!" When the disciples heard this, they fell to the ground and were overcome by fear. But Jesus came and touched them, saying, "Get up and do not be afraid." (Matt. 17:3–8)

After the disciples "fell to the ground and were overcome by fear" at the Transfiguration, Jesus went directly to them. He touched them and said, "Get up and do not be afraid." By this point the Transfiguration was over. Jesus' face no longer shone like the sun; his clothing was no longer dazzlingly white; Moses and Elijah were gone. Only Jesus was there with them, and he wanted them to stand up, to get on their feet. They would soon be returning from their mountaintop experience to face new challenges and threats.

Some leaders seem to thrive on intimidation, exploiting the fears and weaknesses of others to increase their power and control, trying to make themselves stronger by making others weaker and keeping them at a disadvantage. Jesus does not want his disciples to be groveling at his feet and he does not want them to be afraid. He frequently comforts the anxious: *Fear not*. Jesus urges his disciples to get off the ground and stand on their own feet.

John Macquarrie once said in a sermon that in the Incarnation the lover takes on a state of equality with the beloved. The eternal Son shares our humanity. And Jesus tells his disciples to *get up*. He will stand with them and be with them through everything they face. In Jesus, the Savior and redeemer of the world, we have been delivered from evil and made "worthy to stand" before God (Eucharistic Prayer B, BCP, 368). In Jesus, we can stand before God at the Eucharist; we can stand in the face of opposition; we can stand when we have fallen. We can stand when confused, overwhelmed, or afraid. Jesus loves us, strengthens us to stand, and urges us to *get up!*

Questions to ponder

1. When have you been confused, overwhelmed, or afraid?
2. What helped you to get up, to get back on your feet?
3. Did you find Christ present? Did you find new strength?
4. Have you helped someone else to stand when they had fallen?

Pray with Me

Come quickly, dear Lord; help us when we fall. Calm our fears, let us find clarity in our confusion, guide us to find our way forward when we are lost and overwhelmed. Be with us always. Strengthen us to stand; move us to get up!

Twenty-Seven

Who is my neighbor?

Jesus replied, "A man was going down from Jerusalem to Jericho, and fell into the hands of robbers, who stripped him, beat him, and went away, leaving him half dead. Now by chance a priest was going down that road; and when he saw him, he passed by on the other side. So likewise a Levite, when he came to the place and saw him, passed by on the other side. But a Samaritan while traveling came near him; and when he saw him, he was moved with pity. He went to him and bandaged his wounds, having poured oil and wine on them. Then he put him on his own animal, brought him to an inn, and took care of him. The next day he took out two denarii, gave them to the innkeeper, and said, 'Take care of him; and when I come back, I will repay you whatever more you spend.' Which of these three, do you think, was a neighbor to the man who fell into the hands of the robbers?" [The lawyer] said, "The one who showed him mercy." Jesus said to him, "Go and do likewise." (Luke 10:29–37)

A lawyer tries to test Jesus, perhaps to see if he can really answer the most important question: How can we inherit eternal life? Jesus

Who is my neighbor? 239

turns the question back on the lawyer, asking him what is his interpretation. The lawyer in response gives the correct answer: Love God and love your neighbor. When Jesus tells him to do likewise, the lawyer becomes defensive. *Who is my neighbor?* he wonders. What does it even mean to have a neighbor, or to be a neighbor for someone? How can I know what my responsibility is? A legal argument against Jesus' teaching on loving the neighbor could be it was "void for vagueness"—too vague to be understood or applied.

Jesus tells a parable to quickly resolve any doubt concerning vagueness in his teaching about how to be a good neighbor and love a neighbor. The traveler is attacked by bandits, beaten, robbed, and abandoned with injuries on the road from Jerusalem to Jericho. No help is offered by the religious leaders who leave him alone and helpless. Dr. Martin Luther King Jr. once visited this road and stated that even today it is a desolate place of vulnerability for travelers: "Many sudden curves provide likely places for ambushing and expose the traveler to unforeseen attacks. Long ago the road was known as the Bloody Pass" (King, "On Being a Good Neighbor," in *Strength to Love*).

Finally a Samaritan sees the wounded traveler, and he stops to help. This story would have shocked Jesus' audience because Samaritans were not well respected in Jesus' day. The Jews considered them to be heathens, an inferior people. And yet it was a Samaritan who provided abundant care for the helpless, half-dead traveler. The Samaritan stopped to help when the others kept going. He took the injured man to a safe place to recover and paid his cost at the inn. Even though the traveler was a stranger and apparently not a kinsman, the Samaritan recognized him as a neighbor. The Samaritan was a good neighbor for him.

There are many ways to be a good neighbor. Segregation in public places such as swimming pools was outlawed in the United States by the

1964 Civil Rights Act, but desegregation was resisted strongly in some places. In 1969 Fred Rogers, the creator and star of public television's *Mister Rogers' Neighborhood,* aired a brief segment in which his character, Mr. Rogers, invited the local policeman, Officer Clemmons, played by François Clemmons, to share a wading pool and soak their feet in cold water on a hot day. Mr. Rogers' bare feet were already in the wading pool, and Officer Clemmons took off his boots and socks to put his feet side by side with Mr. Rogers' feet in the shallow water. Mr. Rogers was White, Officer Clemmons was Black. It was a beautiful day in the neighborhood. It was an epiphany. This was one of the most memorable television segments of a program that ran for over thirty years. On that day Mr. Rogers and Officer Clemmons were good neighbors for each other, and Fred Rogers was a good neighbor for the country. His program and witness remind us that we stand as neighbors—to help and be helped, to love and be loved—by everyone loved by our Lord. Mr. Rogers would frequently ask, "Will you be my neighbor?" (without exclusions).

Questions to ponder

1. Who are your neighbors? What blessings do you receive from your neighbors?
2. Have you helped and shown concern for your neighbors?
3. Do you find Christ present in the love you share with your neighbors?
4. Do you see the world differently when you recognize your neighbors?
5. What does it mean for you to be a good neighbor?

Pray with me

God of mercy, Lord of our hearts, help us to be good neighbors. Move us to reach out in love for all our neighbors, everyone you love. Help us to love them and ourselves. Let us know your love in us as we share generously with others. May our hearts, souls, strength, and minds be available and offered in love for you; let our love for others reflect our love for you.

References

Anselm, *Why God Became Man,* trans. Janet Fairweather, in *Anselm of Canterbury: The Major Works, Oxford World's Classics,* ed. Brian Davies and G. R. Evans (Oxford: Oxford University Press, 1998), 260–356.

Thomas Aquinas, *Summa Contra Gentiles, Book Three: Providence, Part I,* trans. Vernon J. Bourke (Notre Dame, IN: University of Notre Dame Press, 1975), 73 (3:17 [8]).

Athanasius, *On the Incarnation (De Incarnatione Verbi Dei),* in *A Select Library of Nicene and Post-Nicene Fathers of the Christian Church, Second Series,* vol. 4, *St. Athanasius: Select Works and Letters,* ed. Philip Schaff and Henry Wace (Grand Rapids, MI: Eerdmans, 1971), 65.

Augustine, *Confessions,* trans. R. S. Pine-Coffin (Harmondsworth, England: Penguin, 1961), 21 (I, 1).

Benedict, *The Rule of Saint Benedict,* ed. Timothy Fry, O.S.B. (New York: Vintage, 1988), 3.

William Blake, "Visions of the Daughters of Albion," in *The Complete Poetry and Prose of William Blake,* ed. David V. Erdman (Berkeley and Los Angeles: University of California Press, 1982), 51. Blake, "Jerusalem," in *Complete Poetry and Prose of William Blake,* 258.

Dietrich Bonhoeffer, *The Cost of Discipleship,* trans. R. H. Fuller, Irmgard Booth (New York: Touchstone, 1995), 45, 66.

Raymond Brown, *An Introduction to the New Testament* (New York: Doubleday, 1997), 361.

Robert M. Cooper, "The Fantasy of Control," *St. Luke's Journal of Theology* 33 (September 1990): 259–69.

244 References

Dorothy Day, *All the Way to Heaven: The Selected Letters of Dorothy Day,* ed. Robert Ellsberg (New York: Image Books, 2010), 480, 285, 332.

James DeKoven, "Gathering Up the Fragments," in *Sermons Preached on Various Occasions* (New York: D. Appleton, 1880), 310–319.

Charles Dickens, *A Christmas Carol* (Croxley Green, Hertfordshire, UK: Chiltern, 2020), 100–101.

T. S. Eliot, "The Dry Salvages," in *Four Quartets* (New York: Harcourt, Brace, 1943), 41 (lines 132–140).

Austin Farrer, *The Glass of Vision* (Westminster, UK: Dacre Press, 1948), 33.

James E. Griffiss, "Meditations on the Idols of our Temptation," in *A Silent Path to God* (Philadelphia: Fortress Press, 1980), 87–108.

Ignatius of Loyola, *The Spiritual Exercises,* in *Ignatius of Loyola: The Spiritual Exercises and Selected Works,* ed. George E. Ganss, S.J. (New York and Mahwah, NJ: Paulist Press, 1991), 201–205.

Terrence G. Kardong, *Benedict's Rule: A Translation and Commentary* (Collegeville, MN: Liturgical Press, 1996), 421, 558.

Martin Luther King Jr., "Remaining Awake Through a Great Revolution," in *A Testament of Hope: The Essential Writings of Martin Luther King Jr.,* ed. James M. Washington (New York: HarperCollins, 1986), 277.

Martin Luther King Jr., *I Have a Dream: Writings and Speeches that Changed the World,* ed. James Melvin Washington (New York: HarperCollins, 1992), 102–106.

Martin Luther King Jr., "On Being a Good Neighbor," in *Strength to Love* (Minneapolis: Fortress Press, 2010), 26.

Maxwell King, *The Good Neighbor: The Life and Work of Fred Rogers* (New York: Abrams Press, 2018), 206.

Karl Menninger, Martin Mayman, and Paul Pruyser, *The Vital Balance: The Life Process in Mental Health and Illness* (New York: Viking Press, 1963), 406–417.

Julian of Norwich, *Revelations of Divine Love (Short Text and Long Text),* trans. Elizabeth Spearing (London: Penguin, 1998), 89 [The Long Text, chapters 34–35].

References   245

William J. Schneider, *American Martyr: The Jon Daniels Story* (Harrisburg, PA: Morehouse Publishing, 1992), 110.

Robert Boak Slocum, "A Heart for the Future," in *A Heart for the Future: Writings on the Christian Hope,* ed. Robert Boak Slocum (New York: Church Publishing, 2004), 29.

Robert Boak Slocum, "Divine Action and Human Freedom," in *Light in a Burning-Glass: A Systematic Presentation of Austin Farrer's Theology* (Columbia, SC: University of South Carolina Press, 2007), 77–88.

Robert B. Slocum, "Geoffrey Studdert-Kennedy ('Woodbine Willie'): The Crucified God," *Modern Believing* 58, no. 3 (2017): 217–242, https://doi.org/10.3828/mb.2017.17.

Robert B. Slocum, "Jonathan Daniels: Faith, Freedom, and Sacrifice," *Anglican and Episcopal History* 89, no. 2 (June 2020): 109–122.

Robert B. Slocum, "Magi," *Anglican Theological Review* 84, no. 1 (Winter 2002): 133.

Robert B. Slocum, "Thrown into God's Arms: The Sacrificial Grace of Dietrich Bonhoeffer," *Journal of Ecumenical Studies* 58, no. 1 (Winter, 2023): 16–30.

William Stringfellow, *A Simplicity of Faith: My Experience in Mourning* (Nashville, TN: Abingdon, 1982), 89–90.

Geoffrey Anketell Studdert-Kennedy, *The Hardest Part* (London: Hodder and Soughton, 1918), 4–5.

Joan Gale Thomas, *If Jesus Came to My House* (Eugene, OR: Wipf and Stock, 2018 Allegro, 1951).

Miroslav Volf, "The Final Reconciliation: Reflections on a Social Dimension of the Eschatological Transition," in *A Heart for the Future,* ed. Robert Boak Slocum (Eugene, OR: Wipf and Stock, 2018), 233–234.

Stanley Weintraub, *Silent Night, the Story of the World War I Christmas Truce* (New York: Penguin, 2002), 143, 175.

www.ingramcontent.com/pod-product-compliance
Lightning Source LLC
Jackson TN
JSHW081113260725
88309JS00003B/6